IS THERE DEATH AFTER LIFE?

MARK H. GRAESER

•

JOHN A. LYNN

•

JOHN W. S

D0862962

NOTE: All Scripture quoted in this book is from the King James Version unless otherwise noted. Words in all **bold** letters indicate our added emphasis. Words inside brackets within quotes or verses are also our additions.

"Scripture quotations marked (NIV) are taken from THE HOLY BIBLE, NEW INTERNATIONAL VERSION. Copyright © 1973, 1978, 1984 International Bible Society. Used by permission of Zondervan Publishers."

The sacred name of God, *Yahweh*, is indicated by "LORD"

ISBN # 0-9628971-0-8
FIFTH EDITION
© 1991, 1992, 1993, 1996, 2004

To receive our bimonthly newsletter, *The Sower*, and a complete listing of our materials please contact us at:

CHRISTIAN EDUCATIONAL SERVICES
(Referred to in footnotes as "CES")
2144 East 52nd Street
Indianapolis, Indiana 46205
888-255-6189, M-F 8:30 to 5
Fax: 317-255-6249
CES@CESonline.org
www.CESonline.org

Christian Educational Services is a division of Spirit & Truth Fellowship International

For further study we recommend you to visit our research website:
www.TruthOrTradition.com
Dedicated to helping you understand the Word of God,
free from the traditions of men.

Printed in the United States of America

TABLE OF CONTENTS

Acknowledgments

To Bob Strouss, for suggesting what we feel is just the right title for this book.

To Jim Brandyberry, for his significant contribution of information and insight regarding Church history and the influx of Greek philosophy regarding the state of the dead.

To Bill Barton, for his valuable assistance in editing this manuscript.

To Steve Lortz, for his help in editing and compiling the Scripture Index.

To Joe Ramon, for his service in almost singlehandedly revising the entire layout of the book for the second edition, and for his assistance in the third edition.

To Pat Lynn, for her most diligent efforts in typing our manuscript and its countless revisions. She also contributed valuable editorial advice and helped with layout and design.

Preface

It was once said with tongue in cheek that "religion" introduces a person to the subject of death and then keeps reminding him about it until he experiences it firsthand. Actually, every person, religious or not, is from the early years of his life well aware of the inescapable reality of his death. British poet Thomas Chatterton once remarked, "I have been at war with the grave for some time, and I find it not so easy to vanquish it as I imagined. We can find asylum to hide from every creditor but that."

God never intended for there to be a dead end on the road of life. Through Jesus Christ, He has made available the antidote to death, which is life—*everlasting* life. Rather than simply believe what God's Word says about death and its aftermath, many people have concocted their own doctrines regarding this horrible, inescapable tragedy.

Such doctrines fall into the category of "religion," which is man's own ideas and traditions about God and the deep issues of life. Unfortunately, the religious traditions of men have for many people long superseded the words of God. Jesus confronted the religious leaders of his day, saying, "...Ye do err, not knowing the scriptures, nor the power of God" (Matthew 22:29); "...Why do ye also transgress the commandment of God by your tradition" (Matthew 15:3); and "...ye made the commandment of God of none effect by your tradition" (Matthew 15:6).

So it is with the many traditions and beliefs regarding the subject of life after death that are in vogue today. Man-made, they do not provide a true answer to the question in each person's heart: "What happens to me when I die?" It is truth, not tradition, that sets one free, as Jesus stated (John 8:32). Conversely, error regarding important spiritual matters enslaves people. Apart from the truth, we are besieged with many confusing and often frightening theories.

The Word of God states that many "...through fear of death were all their lifetime subject to bondage" (Hebrews 2:15). This bondage is often due to one's fear of the unknown. In His wisdom and mercy, our benevolent Creator knew that we would experience such emotion. In keeping with His desire to provide man with "...all things that *pertain* unto life and godliness..." (2 Peter 1:3), He has provided answers to the many unsettling questions regarding the topic of death. He has stated in His Word that He does not want us "...ignorant, brethern, concerning them which are asleep [dead]..." (1 Thessalonians 4:13).

Speaking about the written Word of God, Jesus Christ said, "...thy word is truth" (John 17:17). When it comes to spiritual things beyond the realm of man's five senses, such as life after death, the Word of God is the *only* credible witness. In stark contrast to the vague, groundless theories and speculations originating in the minds of men, God, the Author of life, presents clear, straightforward answers to the most profound questions of the human heart. Thus we must look into God's Word, the literature of eternity, and let Him speak for Himself about the deep issues of life and death.

The Bible is the standard of all literature, and God the Author of all authors. As literature, it contains a rich variety of linguistic thoughts, expressions and usages. Like any author, God has the right to use language as He deems appropriate to His purposes. E.W. Bullinger, an eminent British Bible scholar (1837-1913), identified the use of more than 200 figures of speech in the Bible. These figures greatly enrich its literary value and at the same time entrust its readers with great responsibility.

Those who endeavor to study, understand and interpret the Bible must become very sensitive to the literary devices it employs, because its study is not merely for cultural amusement. Our very lives, both temporal and eternal, depend on an accurate understanding of God's words, which are the very "words of life."

When God makes statements of fact, or uses language in the way it is normally used, we should surely take note. When He departs from customary usage of words, syntax, grammar and statements true to fact, we must take double note, for such departures serve to better communicate truth than can literal statements of fact.

As the only credible witness of eternal and spiritual verities, the Bible gives testimony in a variety of ways—some literal, some figurative. Misconstruing the use of its language is one of the principle errors of the orthodox Christian Church, particularly, as we shall see, regarding the state of the dead. This has resulted in the Word of God being twisted, distorted and misrepresented.

vi

The real source of all that is contrary to God's Word is His archenemy, the Devil. He was the first to minimize the grim reality of death, and his original lie, "...Ye shall not surely die" (Genesis 3:4), is still being propounded. Millions have been duped into believing that everlasting life is not conditional upon obedience to the Word of God, but is inherent within all men no matter what they believe.

Although most ancient pagan religions, such as those of the Babylonians and Egyptians, believed in some form of immediate life after death, the ancient Greeks were the first to philosophize that each man has an "immortal soul." The refrain caught on, and by the third century it had been harmonized into a watered-down Christianity, despite its complete antithesis to Scripture. Over the centuries, corollary falsehoods have been attached to this grievous error. The most harmful are (1) that God is responsible for death and (2) that all unbelievers will be eternally tormented.

Tragically, the vast majority of so-called "orthodox," "fundamental," "Bible-believing," "mainline," "evangelical" Christian churches has embraced and traditionalized these false doctrines. While Christians should have been proclaiming the biblical truths that death is an enemy, that the Devil is its author and that eternal life is conditional upon a believer being raised from the dead by Jesus Christ at His appearing, most have not.

Instead, they have joined the ranks of the "spiritists," "spiritualists" and nearly all non-Christian religions in teaching that those who have died are not really dead. Sadly typical is the incredible statement made recently by a radio preacher that "When a Christian dies, he has just begun to live." How ironic it is that this error has also greatly helped the cause of millions of proponents of "New Age" doctrine, which fundamental Christianity so vehemently denounces.

Both Christians and non-Christians are teaching that death is merely a transition or "graduation" into a higher realm of consciousness. Thus it is little wonder that the world is absolutely inundated with movies, music, literature and countless quotes by politicians, movie stars, sports heroes and other public figures promulgating this false doctrine. Calling death a "graduation" or the beginning of real life almost makes it alluring and thus opens up sincere people's minds and lives to the forces of evil and their destructive influences. It also makes the Word of God "of none effect."

We are not the first, nor are we the only ones at present, to go against the grain of so-called "orthodoxy" and herald the truth of God's Word regarding this vital subject. Our work contains many references to other men's works, both pro and con, that go into more detail on certain issues. We encourage you to study in greater depth those things that interest you.

Our goal in producing this work is not to offend other Christians, but to glorify the One True God and His Son Jesus Christ and to help God's precious people, many of whom have "...a zeal for God, but not according to knowledge" (Romans 10:2). To do so, we are bound to speak the truth in love. May our sincere effort be found acceptable in the sight of God and serve to make known the truth of His Word.

It is our prayer that this book helps satisfy your hunger and thirst for the truth. We know it is not perfect, but we trust it will enlighten you in regard to that which *is* perfect, the Word of God. We pray also that it will inspire you to both search the Scriptures and share with others the truth you find there. We love you dearly and welcome any further insight you may have on this subject.

2 Peter 1:2

Grace and peace be multiplied unto you through the knowledge of God, and of Jesus our Lord.

MARK H. GRAESER
JOHN A. LYNN
JOHN W. SCHOENHEIT

Introduction

The subject of the state of the dead affects the deepest issues of the hearts of Christian believers, such as our conception of God and His love, our understanding of our salvation and eternal destiny, our lifestyle, our evangelistic efforts and our will to live. Also at stake in this study is the most fundamental of Christian values—our faith in the integrity and credibility of the Bible.

Certain basic questions are usually raised by the mystery of death. Among them are:

(1) What is the "soul"?
(2) What is death?
(3) Where are the dead?
(4) In what state of being are they?
(5) When will this state end?

Traditionally, the orthodox Church has taught that the human "soul" is immortal. Thus it survives death, which affects only the physical body. The soul goes consciously either to "heaven," to be in the presence of God, or to "hell," a place where the soul is aware of separation from God and is tormented for eternity. However, upon careful study, it is clear that Scripture says differently. In fact, there is not one verse in the Bible that speaks of anyone who has died being alive in heaven with Jesus Christ.

The accurate biblical answer to the above questions can be expressed in this statement:

> *The dead are truly dead in "gravedom," and are "sleeping" until the coming of Christ, when He will awaken them.*

Before we present biblical and historical evidence we believe leads to this conclusion, we will first consider some of the consequences of believing Satan's original lie and then set forth the truth of God's Word as it answers the above questions. There *is* death after life, but because God so loved mankind that He gave His only begotten Son, Jesus Christ, and raised Him from the dead, there is also life after death for those who believe on Him. Each and every Christian has the great hope of everlasting life with his heavenly Father, his Lord Jesus Christ and all who have believed in them.

We realize the doctrine that the dead are conscious in eternity is usually taught sincerely by well-meaning Christians, often in an attempt to comfort the bereaved upon the loss of loved ones. Nevertheless, we encourage those who hold this traditional position to reconsider it in the light of Scriptural truth, which in the end will prove vastly more comforting, satisfying and uplifting than "the doctrines and commandments of men."

CHAPTER ONE

Consequences of Believing Satan's Lie

The Father of Lies

Among other things, Jesus Christ came to expose Satan's methods. Chief among these is the Devil's consistent contradiction of God's Word.

John 8:44

> Ye are of *your* father the devil, and the lusts of your father ye will do. He was a murderer from the beginning, and abode not in the truth, because there is no truth in him. When he speaketh a lie, he speaketh of his own: for he is a liar, and the father of it.

In John 10:10a, Jesus clearly revealed Satan's intentions: "The thief cometh not, but for to steal, and to kill, and to destroy...." Satan's ultimate goal is to promote death and destruction, as the Bible makes clear.

Hebrews 2:14 (NIV)

Since the children have flesh and blood, he too shared in their
humanity so that by his death he might destroy him who holds
the power of death—that is, the devil.

The Devil holds the power of death, and one of his most effective
aids in exercising this power is the lie that death is in reality the
gateway to everlasting life and ultimate wisdom. He first told this lie early
in Genesis.

Perhaps you recall that Satan's first recorded utterance in
Scripture was a challenge to the veracity of God's Word. Satan said,
"...Did God really say, 'You must not eat from any tree in the garden?'"
(Genesis 3:1-NIV). This deceptive misquote of God's revealed Word led
to his second utterance, "...Ye shall not surely die" (Genesis 3:4), which
was just the opposite of what God had said to Adam.

Genesis 2:16 and 17

(16) And the LORD God commanded the man, saying, Of every
tree of the garden thou mayest freely eat:

(17) But of the tree of the knowledge of good and evil, thou shalt
not eat of it: for in the day that thou eatest thereof thou shalt
surely die.

God said, "...thou shalt surely die." Satan said, "...Ye shall not
surely die." Scripture makes clear who was telling the truth.

Romans 5:12

Wherefore, as by one man [Adam] sin entered into the world,
and death by sin; and so death passed upon all men, for that all
have sinned.

Death, both spiritual and physical, was the result of man's believing
Satan's lie. The idea that there is really no such thing as death is still being

promoted today, even within the Christian Church. Satan's purpose has remained the same: to promote the idea that humans do not actually die, but go on living after their death whether they believe God's Word or not. In this way, he obscures the light of the good news of Christ and His resurrection, one's only hope of deliverance from death unto everlasting life.

False Hope

The false doctrine that the dead are alive and already in heaven or hell is so well entrenched in the average Christian's mind that he has probably never considered its harmful ramifications. Understanding that Satan is the "father" of this lie explains why the consequences of believing it are so serious. The first, and perhaps most serious, consequence of believing this doctrine is that it changes the Christian's focus from the appearing of the Prince of Life, Jesus Christ, to the coming of one's own death.

In 1829, the Scottish Bible scholar Edward Irving, in a lecture entitled "The Second Advent of Our Lord," stated that:

> ... instead of looking to that glorious event [the Lord's appearing], and to all the circumstances connected therewith, the church has nearly forgotten it, and instead of it, to take up with miserable substitutes, such as that every man should think but of the day of his death; from which consideration there comes not joy nor strength, but weakness and oppression.... [1]

In contrast, the late Dr. Walter Martin, a noted Christian apologist, in his epochal work *The Kingdom of the Cults*, which well represents the position of orthodox Christianity on this subject, wrote:

---

[1] Edward Irving, "The Second Advent of Our Lord, and His Everlasting Kingdom," *Five Lectures* (Lecture V) (John Bennett, London, England, 1835), pp. 52-60.

The great hope of the believer, then, is the joy of personal union with the Lord, and this union, the Apostle Paul tells us, takes place at the death of the body. [2]

How sad it is to teach God's people that the hope of a Christian is his own death, and how opposed to God's perspective that death is an "enemy," as 1 Corinthians 15:26 clearly states: "The last enemy *that* shall be destroyed is death." Biblically, death is a thief, not a benefactor. Death *takes away* life; it does not *give* a greater life.

In attempting to preserve the traditions of historic, orthodox Christianity, such teaching that the "dead" are "alive" blatantly contradicts God's Word and further entrenches the Christian church in this error. Those who have mistakenly propounded this doctrine have apparently overlooked the many verses plainly stating that the focal point of a Christian's hope is not his own death, but the appearing of our Lord Jesus Christ from heaven. For example:

John 14:2 and 3

(2) In my Father's house are many mansions: if *it were* not *so*, I would have told you. I go to prepare a place for you.

(3) And if I go and prepare a place for you, **I will come again**, and receive you unto myself; that where *I* am, *there ye* may be also.

1 Thessalonians 2:19

For what *is* our hope, or joy, or crown of rejoicing? *Are* not even *ye* in the presence of our Lord Jesus Christ **at his coming**?

1 Thessalonians 4:16 and 17

(16) For the Lord himself shall **descend from heaven** with a shout, with the voice of the archangel, and with the trump of God: and the dead in Christ shall rise first:

---

[2] Dr. Walter Martin, *The Kingdom of the Cults* (Zondervan Publishing Co., Grand Rapids, Michigan, 1965), p. 389.

(17) Then we which are alive *and* remain shall be caught up together with them in the clouds, **to meet the Lord in the air**: and so shall we ever be with the Lord.

Titus 2:13

Looking for that blessed hope, and the glorious **appearing** of the great God and our Saviour Jesus Christ;

It is the occasion of Christ's appearing from heaven that Christians should anticipate as the way of deliverance from the bondage and corruption of death. Jesus Christ is the only gateway to everlasting life and the only means by which believers will have access to God's presence in Paradise.[3] When Jesus Christ comes again, He will fashion new, glorious bodies for us (Philippians 3:21). Apart from having these new bodies, there is no hope of entrance into the presence of God. Near the end of his life, the Apostle Paul wrote the following about this occasion:

2 Timothy 4:8

Henceforth there is laid up for me a crown of righteousness, which the Lord, the righteous judge, shall give me **at that day**: and not to me only, but unto all them also that love his appearing.

Shifting the event that triggers our entrance into the presence of God from Christ's appearing to our own death is nothing short of satanic subterfuge. In the minds of many, Satan has subtly changed the gateway to eternal life from Jesus Christ to death itself. Considering the past actions of God's archenemy, this clever trick is totally consistent with his methods. The Christian's hope is not death, but the appearing of Jesus Christ. When He appears, each Christian who is still alive will exchange his mortal body for a glorious immortal body, and each believer who has died will be raised to glorious and everlasting life.

---

[3] For more information, hear CES Mar/Apr 1992 Tape, "The Kingdom of God: Paradise Regained."

Who Needs Resurrection?

A second consequence of believing the doctrine that the dead are alive is one that has drastic implications for biblical integrity and harmony. Believing that all the dead are conscious in heaven or hell reduces the great truth of resurrection to virtual insignificance. Death must be *true* death if resurrection is to be meaningful. If death involves only the body, with the soul and/or consciousness living on, then resurrection has lost *at least* half its significance.

If all believers have gone into the presence of God at their deaths, the monumental importance of Jesus Christ's resurrection is negated. If Abraham, David, Job and others were already in heaven as disembodied souls or spirits, enjoying the presence of God in "eternity," then our enemy, death, had already been vanquished before Christ's resurrection, and eternal life was available without Christ. In fact, if it were true, as many teach, that Enoch, Elijah and Moses went to heaven bodily, then Jesus is not even the only human in heaven with a body. Such teaching contradicts the Word of God, confuses sincere Christians and dilutes their joy of hope.

It also leads to a question posed by Wycliffe, Tyndale, Luther and others during the course of Christian history. If disembodied souls are able to live and enjoy the presence of God in heaven for eternity, then what is the need for a resurrection?

William Tyndale (1492-1536), the heroic Reformation figure chiefly responsible for translating the Bible into English, wrote the following to combat the teaching of the Roman Catholic Church:

> And when he [Sir Thomas More] proveth that the saints be in heaven in glory with Christ already, saying 'If God be their god, they be in heaven for he is not the God of the dead ...' therewith he stealeth away Christ's argument wherewith he proveth the resurrection, that Abraham and all the saints shall rise again, and not that their souls were in heaven, which doctrine was not yet in the world, and with this doctrine he [More] taketh away the resurrection quite, and maketh Christ's argument of none effect.
>
> And in like manner Paul's argument to the Corinthians is worth naught. For when he sayeth, 'If there be no resurrection we be of all wretches the most miserable ...' I marvel that Paul had not comforted the Thessalonians with that doctrine if he had

[known] of it that the souls of their dead had been in joy, as he did with the resurrection that their souls should rise again. If the souls be in heaven in as great glory as the angels after your doctrine, show me what cause should be of resurrection. [4]

Tyndale went on:

And you in putting them [the souls of the dead] in heaven, hell and purgatory, destroy the arguments wherewith Christ and Paul prove the resurrection ... the true faith putteth the resurrection which we are warned to look for every hour. The heathen philosophers, denying that, did put that the souls did ever live. And the Pope joineth this spiritual doctrine of the philosophers together, things so contrary that they cannot agree. [5]

If a body is not required for life in the "hereafter," then God is going to a lot of trouble for no apparent reason by "reuniting" everyone with his body. And the physical death and resurrection of Jesus Christ, serving only to allow the disembodied soul or spirit to be united with a body that it obviously can do without, seems to be of little significance.

The teaching that the soul lives on after death destroys the uniqueness of Christian doctrine, that is, that Jesus Christ's bodily resurrection is prerequisite to anyone being given everlasting life. With so much biblical emphasis on the resurrection of Jesus Christ, any doctrine undermining it is highly suspect.

That Sounds "Familiar"

A third consequence of believing the doctrine that souls live on after the body dies is that it plays into the hands of those who promote the practice of communicating with the dead. Today many people, both Christian and non-Christian, attempt to communicate with the spirits of

---

[4] "An Answer To Sir Thomas More's Dialogue 1530," from *The Black Letter Manuscript* in the British Museum.

[5] Ibid.

the dead, often in seances or via "channeling." Such practices are similar to ancestor worship, historically a practice of most non-Christian religions. Pagans believe that the spirits of departed ancestors intervene in their lives, both for good and evil. Thus, as godlike beings, they must be worshiped and entreated. Superstition and fear of the unknown are always hallmarks of such false doctrine.

If there really are "departed souls" or "spirits" that are conscious and have knowledge of eternity or other matters of interest to those of us still earthbound, why not communicate with them? Because they are not there to answer. What *will* answer are evil spirits (fallen angels currently under Satan's dominion) impersonating the dead. In the Old Testament, however, God expressly forbade communication with such "familiar spirits." For example:

Leviticus 19:31

Regard not them that have familiar spirits, neither seek after wizards, to be defiled by them: I *am* the LORD your God.

Leviticus 20:6

And the soul that turneth after such as have familiar spirits, and after wizards, to go a whoring after them, I will even set my face against that soul, and will cut him off from among his people.

Deuteronomy 18:10 and 11

(10) There shall not be found among you *any one* that maketh his son or his daughter to pass through the fire, *or* that useth divination, *or* an observer of times, or an enchanter, or a witch,

(11) Or a charmer, or a consulter with familiar spirits, or a wizard, or a necromancer.

2 Kings 23:24

Moreover the *workers with* familiar spirits, and the wizards, and the images, and the idols, and all the abominations that were spied in the land of Judah and in Jerusalem, did Josiah put away, that he might perform the words of the law which were written in the book that Hilkiah the priest found in the house of the LORD.

They are called "familiar spirits" because these evil spirits are familiar with people who have died and can even reproduce their likenesses and personalities as if they were still alive in the realm of the "hereafter." [6] The judgment of God against Saul, Israel's first king, that led to his death was in part caused by his attempt to divine the LORD's will through a familiar spirit impersonating Samuel (1 Samuel 28:3-11; 1Chronicles 10:13 and 14). It is appalling that the orthodox Christian position cites this record as evidence that the dead can appear and communicate to the living. [7] (For further explanation of this record, see Chapter Seven.)

Sometimes a familiar spirit will appear to a person who is not actively seeking to contact the dead. Although such experiences are very convincing to those who see what appears to be a dead friend or relative, God's Word exposes this counterfeit as another satanic attempt to convince people that the dead are actually still alive.

Scripture makes it plain that contacting the dead is a sin forbidden by God. Surely those supposedly living in heaven with God would not sin by initiating or participating in contact with the living.

There is nothing in the New Testament that changes God's Old Testament prohibition against attempting to communicate with the dead. The reason for this is simple: The dead are unconscious in "gravedom" and cannot communicate with the living. If anything is communicated, it will be from evil spirits attempting to deceive people into accepting that the dead have not "surely died."

Before her death in 1970, Eileen Garrett was for more than thirty years one of America's greatest mediums. What did those spirits that spoke through her want to communicate? "Their primary mission seemed to be to prove the survival of human consciousness beyond death." [8] Acceptance of the doctrine that the dead are alive and can be communicated with may very well be the first step toward allowing such spirits into one's life, making possible all manner of destructive results.

In their book, *America, The Sorcerer's New Apprentice*, Dave Hunt and T.A. McMahon rightly observe that "one of mankind's most compelling fascinations in every culture throughout history has been to

---

[6] For more information on this subject, the reader is referred to: Raphael Gasson, *The Challenging Counterfeit* (Logos International, Plainfield, New Jersey, 1966).

[7] Martin, op. cit., *The Kingdom of the Cults*, p. 391.

[8] Dave Hunt and T.A. McMahon, *America, The Sorcerer's New Apprentice* (Harvest House, Eugene, Oregon, 1988), p. 172.

communicate with the dead. Mediumship is one of the world's oldest professions and has always been an integral part of nature religion in its many forms." [9]

The authors also quote from an article by Andrew Greeley in the January/February 1987 issue of *American Health Magazine*, entitled "Mysticism Goes Mainstream": "Nearly one-half of American adults (42 percent) now believe they have been in contact with someone who has died." [10] Hunt and McMahon comment that the figure of 42 percent represented nearly a 60 percent increase from a previous poll eleven years earlier and state: "Any disease showing statistics like that would be recognized as epidemic." [11]

Death: Friend or Foe?

A fourth consequence of believing the doctrine of immediate entrance into heaven at death, and the corollary teaching that death is God's will, is that it may subtly undermine a Christian's will to live by causing him to accept death as a "friend." But God's Word is clear:

1 Corinthians 15:26

The last **enemy** *that* shall be destroyed *is* death.

If a person is persuaded that death is a "friend" that will introduce him to the glories of eternity, he may adopt a cavalier attitude toward his own death. Satan can then wield the power of death more easily, manipulating the untimely death of his victims by fatal disease, murder, suicide or accident.

Why should a Christian aggressively cling to life on earth and endeavor to live it to the fullest when a much brighter and higher existence awaits him with God "on the other side"? Does this teaching motivate a Christian to behave in a manner that will cause him to prolong,

---

[9] Ibid., p. 188.

[10] Ibid., p. 109.

[11] Ibid., p. 110.

preserve and enjoy his earthly existence and service to God? To the contrary, one's belief in an immediate afterlife might even cause him to hasten his own death. In fact, history contains a great many records of Christians who have committed suicide so that they could "be with Jesus." Tragically, they have often taken others with them to the grave by murdering them first.

One effect of this false doctrine may possibly be seen in the context of a serious illness. It is generally understood that an individual with a strong will to live is more likely to survive a life-threatening illness. How ironic that Christian believers who have access to God's miraculous, supernatural power for deliverance often negate it by a truncated will to live, based on their misunderstanding of the true nature of death. Unbelievers who think that this life is all there is can too often muster more of the innate and God-given instinct for survival than does a child of God. Does it glorify God that His people should have less desire than unbelievers to live as long as they can on earth? Does this help win the lost and persuade them of the benefits of following the way of Jesus Christ?

In the same vein, many Christians are very fatalistic about the moment of their deaths. Perhaps to deal with the fear of death, they assume the Lord already has the day picked. When their "number is up," they will die, regardless of their behavior, thoughts or even prayers. They think that God alone determines the day of their death when *He* is ready.

There is, however, no biblical justification for the idea that the day of one's death is "set in stone." Rather, the Bible is replete with examples of men and women shortening or prolonging their lives by the way they lived— for example, Saul (1 Chronicles 10:13) and Hezekiah (2 Kings 20:1-5).

Although believing that God determines the day of one's death may seem comforting to a misguided believer in, say, an airplane bouncing through turbulence, it actually may work against him. In a critical situation, intense prayer and supplication would be much more beneficial than passively waiting to see what God's will is. It is obvious that our own choices go a long way toward determining what kind of life we live and for how long. Thinking fatalistically, one is probably less likely to do those things that make for a long and healthy life.

If it were true that it is God who determines one's appointed time to die, then death would be a friend, and God would be its cause. Neither is true. God's will for man is a long, healthy and prosperous life as a testimony to His love and goodness (e.g., Proverbs 4:10; 9:11; Ephesians 6:3). Jesus said that He always did the Father's will (John 4:34; 5:30; 6:38; 17:4), and He healed all who came to Him in faith (Matthew 4:23; 8:16; 9:35; Luke 9:11). (Note: For a thorough exposition of the subject of how to biblically reconcile the co-existence of a loving God with evil, sin and suffering, we encourage you to order the book *Don't Blame God!* by the same authors.)

Of course, most Christians who teach that God kills His people seldom say it that way. They usually say, of a Christian who has died, that God "called him home." What an incredible euphemism! Think about it. "Home." What visions the word carries with it: a hot meal, a warm bed, a loving family. But what are people *really* saying about a saint who has died, when they sweetly say that God "called him home"? They're saying that God, Who is love, light and goodness, ran him down with a bus, ate out his insides with cancer or had him beaten to death in an alley. Repulsive? Yes, death is just that.

Although Jack Sharkey, former world heavyweight boxing champion, was hardly known as a spokesman for fundamental Christian orthodoxy, his statement in 1978 upon hearing of the death of his friend, boxer Gene Tunney, is representative of its confusion. Sharkey said that Tunney's death "makes me think it's too bad. We all get along and the good Lord takes us." [12] How can a *good* Lord do *bad* things?

The Word of God clearly states that God is "good" (Mark 10:18) and that death is an "enemy" to His people (1 Corinthians 15:26). God tells us also that it is the Devil who holds the power of death (Hebrews 2:14-NIV) and that the Devil was a "...murderer from the beginning..." (John 8:44).

It should be noted here that although death is of the Devil, this does not mean that a Christian who dies is "bad" or "out of fellowship" or "possessed." Because of the fall of Adam, physical death is the inevitable end of life for each person, unless he is still alive when Christ again appears.

If the Church fails to change its wholly untenable biblical position that the "dead" are actually "alive," it will unwittingly continue to play into the hands of spiritualists, adherents of Eastern mysticism and the proponents of the rapidly growing New Age movement, who deny both the significance of Christ's resurrection and the unique opportunity for

---

[12] *Concord Monitor* (New Hampshire, November 9, 1978), p. 19.

everlasting life through faith in His name. It will also continue to offer people a weak and false hope based on paganism, rather than the comforting and satisfying truth of God's Word.

CHAPTER TWO

What Is the "Soul"?

This Is Your Life

To understand the entire subject of "life after death," it is important to consider the word "soul." Unfortunately, the traditions doctrines and commandments of men have distorted its biblical definition. Though it does have a considerable range of biblical meaning, "soul" cannot be stretched to mean what the Greeks said it meant: "consciousness" or "personality" able to exist apart from the body.

Early in the Bible, God describes man:

Genesis 2:7

...the LORD God formed man *of* the dust of the ground, and breathed into his nostrils the breath of life; and man became a living soul.

In his commentary on the Bible, Dr. Basil F.C. Atkinson states regarding this verse:

It is a mistake to see in this statement the idea that a spiritual nature, akin to the Divine and not shared by the lower creation, was imparted to man. [13]

The Hebrew word translated "soul" in Genesis 2:7 is *nephesh* and is used elsewhere in the Bible for animals as well as man.

Genesis 1:21

And God created great whales, and every living creature [*nephesh*] that moveth, which the waters brought forth abundantly, after their kind, and every winged fowl after his kind: and God saw that *it was* good.

Leviticus 11:46

This *is* the law of the beasts, and of the fowl, and of every living creature [*nephesh*] that moveth in the waters, and of every creature [*nephesh*] that creepeth upon the earth:

Biblically, insects, birds, fish, animals and man have a common life force that animates them. When this is gone, they are dead.

Ecclesiastes 3:19

For that which befalleth the sons of men befalleth beasts; even one thing befalleth them: as the one dieth, so dieth the other; yea, they have all one breath [*ruach*]; so that a man hath no preeminence above a beast....

To say that man is animated by the same life force as all members of the animal kingdom is not to imply that man is merely an animal. God made man in His image and that makes man a unique creation. Only man has the capacity to use language, to reason, to morally discern between

---

[13] Dr. Basil F.C. Atkinson, *Pocket Commentary of the Bible*, (Worthing, Henry Walker, Sussex, England, 1954), p. 31.

right and wrong and so forth. God's purpose in giving man these special attributes was so that man could understand His Word, know Him and love Him.

Several English words in the Bible refer to this life force: "breath," "life," "soul" and "spirit." Precise definitions of and distinctions between the Hebrew words *nephesh* (soul) and *ruach* (spirit) and their New Testament Greek equivalents, *psuche* and *pneuma*, are very difficult to arrive at. They deal with intangible realities, and their biblical usages overlap. Robert L. Whitelaw offers a pertinent analogy:

> Life is *never* spoken of as a substance, least of all a self-conscious entity, added to or removed from the body. Its closest analogy today is in an electric lamp; electricity (still a mystery) converts a mere lamp-structure into a light-giver, yet nothing is added to the lamp when it is turned on, nor removed when it is cut off. So Jesus at death is spoken of in Isaiah 53:8 as "...cut off out of the land of the living...." Life, like electricity, will forever remain a mystery to science in this world. [14]

The soul is the impersonal, temporal, natural life force present in man and is sometimes called "the spirit of man." For example:

James 2:26

> For as the body without the spirit is dead, so faith without works is dead also.

There is nothing in the Hebrew text to connote that "soul" is, by definition, something that can live apart from a body and thus be immortal. Neither is the word "soul" ever used as the "spirit" of the dead. [15] It is most significant that *in the entire Old Testament there is absolutely no mention of a soul going to heaven at death.*

---

[14] Robert L. Whitelaw, "Resurrection Truth: What Is It? And What Does It Forbid?," *Resurrection Magazine* (Fall, 1990), p. 8.

[15] *The New Bible Dictionary* (Wm. B. Eerdmans Publishing, Grand Rapids, Michigan, 1975), p. 1208.

The biblical usage of the Hebrew word *nephesh* (soul) conveys the conception of "the whole person," including his thoughts, feelings, desires and abilities. Via the figure of speech synecdoche, a part put for the whole, the "soul" figuratively represents the whole person, even though literally it is only the life force that animates him. Thus in Scripture, "My soul"= I and "His soul" = He.

There are other figurative usages of *nephesh* that refer to "dead souls," meaning "dead persons" (Leviticus 19:28; Numbers 6:6; Haggai 2:13). Since at death the soul ceases to exist, *nephesh* is figuratively spoken of as going to the grave when it dies.

Psalm 16:10

For Thou wilt not leave my soul in hell [*sheol*= gravedom]; neither wilt thou suffer thine Holy One to see corruption.

Psalm 49:15

But God will redeem my soul from the power of the grave [*sheol*= gravedom]: for he shall receive me. Selah.

Dr. Atkinson again writes that, for many, the meaning of "soul" is:

... derived from the Greeks, chiefly from the great fourth-century [427-347 B.C.] thinker and teacher, Plato, who regarded the soul as a distinct immaterial and immortal entity imprisoned in the body and released from it at death, and carrying the actual human personality. It was in this sense that Plato and the Greeks used the word *psuche*. In the New Testament, however, as in the Septuagint version of the Old Testament, the Greek word [*psuche*], like other prominent terms, is used as is the equivalent word which it translates. The words may be Greek, but the conception is Hebrew. The Old Testament knows nothing of a soul in the Platonic sense. The word *nephesh* means a living animal entity. It may be applied to a human being, in which case it means "person," a sense in which it may still sometimes be used in English. It may be applied to animals in which case it means "creature." [16]

---

[16] Atkinson, op. cit., *Pocket Commentary*, pp. 18 and 19.

It is clear that "the 'soul'... does not stand in dualistic contrast to the body, but signifies man himself whom God seeks and saves for life eternal." [17] (For more information on the word "soul," see Appendix 13 in *The Companion Bible*, edited by E.W. Bullinger.)

It's Greek To Me

The idea of the immortality, or the "eternality," of the soul definitely has its roots in Greek paganism. The Greeks considered the body to be a lower thing than the mind. [18] Once a soul was free from the shackles of the body, it could wing its way into the higher realms of consciousness. The Greeks therefore rejected the notion of a bodily resurrection as needless (see Acts 17:32) and taught that the soul lived on, crossed the river Styx and lived in the land of shades. [19]

One can hardly overemphasize the harmful influence of Greek philosophy upon Christian thought. Consider the following statements from various writers regarding this:

> The strongest force working in favor of a general acceptance of the belief in natural immortality has been the dominant influence of Platonism in the earlier stages of the development of Christian doctrine. [20]

> The notion about the separate state of the soul was an importation into Christianity of the old Greek philosophy. The departed *souls* of the early Christianity were the *shades* of Homer and the Greeks. [21]

---

[17] Karl Hanhart, *The Intermediate State in the New Testament*, (Doctoral dissertation at the University of Amsterdam, Franeker: T. Wever, 1966), pp. 238 and 239.

[18] Charles F. Baker, *Dispensational Theology* (Grace Publications, Grand Rapids, Michigan, 1980 (Third Printing), p. 570.

[19] *New Bible Dictionary*, op. cit., "Resurrection," p. 1086.

[20] *Encyclopedia of Religion and Ethics*, Vol. 1 (Scribner's, New York, 1913), p. 545.

[21] Aaron Ellis, *The Bible vs. Tradition* (The Bible Examiner, New York, 1853), pp. 297 and 298.

But early, a majority of the Christians were Greeks or people more or less Hellenized in thought, so that Greek ideas were bound to assert themselves, especially the Platonic concept of the soul as an indestructible entity. [22]

Many Christian writers of the second and third centuries wanted to show their pagan neighbors the reasonableness of the biblical faith. They wrapped their understanding of Scripture in the robes of philosophy, choosing from the vocabulary of worldly wisdom the words which sparkled and adorned it best. [23]

Church fathers of the first five centuries faced Platonic and neoPlatonic adversaries who denied the Christian resurrection but affirmed the inalienable immortality of the soul. The philosophers themselves disagreed on so me of the fine points. In this setting the apologists reasoned for the bodily resurrection of all men, both good and evil. The common doctrine of the soul's immortality was a convenient tool in handy reach. [24]

The concept of the innate immortality of the soul as a Christian doctrine makes a distinct appearance in patristic literature (that written by those who have come to be known as "the Church Fathers") late in the second century A.D. in the writings of Athenagoras of Alexandria (c. A.D. 127-190). This Greek philosopher converted to Christianity and retained his neoplatonic concept of the nature of man. In defense of Christianity, he endeavored to show that Platonism and the religion of Christ are in fundamental accord. [25] Tertullian of Carthage (c. A.D. 160-240) was another who strongly advocated the immortality of the soul. [26]

The renowned Augustine (A.D. 354-430) expanded upon Tertullianism. Significantly, he had written a book giving sixteen reasons for the immortality of the soul *before* he became a Christian. [27]

---

[22] Clifford H. Moore, *Ancient Beliefs in the Immortality of the Soul* (Cooper Square Publishers, Inc., New York, 1963), p. 71.

[23] Edward Fudge, *The Fire That Consumes* (Providential Press, Houston, Texas 1982), p. 66.

[24] Ibid., p. 75.

[25] Leroy Edwin Froom, *The Conditionalist Faith of Our Fathers* (Vol. 1) (Review and Herald, Washington, D.C., 1965), pp. 928 and 929.

[26] Ibid., p. 951.

[27] Ibid., pp. 1,072 and 1,073.

Augustine offered proofs of immortality that showed his indebtedness to Platonic thought. [28] His Platonic assumption of the inherent immortality of the soul greatly hindered a clear biblical exegesis and consequently set a similar standard for most of Christendom. Regarding Augustine, one writer has commented:

> The evidence in the early Christian writers is clear that much confusion of thought prevailed until Augustine by his genius clarified Christian doctrine through the modified form of Neoplatonism. His system in no slight degree determined the course of thinking within the church on the question of immortality down to the latter part of the 19th century. [29]

The middle ages also was characterized by Platonic emphasis at the expense of the need for resurrection. Foremost in influence among those of that time was Thomas Aquinas (1225-1274), one of the most prominent Roman Catholic theologians of all time. While establishing Aristotelianism as the foundation of "Christian philosophy," Thomas also championed the soul's survival after death and its immediate individual judgment, so that any later judgment was to him but a reaffirmation. [30]

In contrast to the doctrine of the innate immortality of the soul was the doctrine that is today referred to in theological circles as "conditional immortality," that is, that no one will live forever unless Jesus Christ one day gives him everlasting life. This doctrine, which we believe was dominant in the early days of the church because it represents the position of Scripture, virtually disappeared between the fourth and sixteenth centuries. As far as we know now, Lactantius of Nicomedia in Asia Minor (c. 250-330) was the last prominent Christian theologian to hold forth this truth, which was from then on submerged in religious error. [31]

---

[28] Moore, op. cit., *Ancient Beliefs*, p. 122.

[29] Ibid., p. 72.

[30] Milton McC. Gatch, *Death: Meaning and Mortality in Christian Thought and Contemporary Culture* (Seabury Press, New York, 1969), p. 120.

[31] Froom, op. cit., *Conditionalist Faith* (Vol. 2), p. 1,052.

The Reformation: A Near Miss

The doctrine of conditional immortality did not re-surface until the time of the "Reformation," when Martin Luther briefly fished it out. He stated:

> I permit the pope to make articles of faith for himself and his faithful such as ... the soul is immortal, with all those monstrous opinions to be found in the Roman dunghill of decretals. [32]

In France, during the upheaval of the Reformation, some of those known as "Anabaptists" rejected John Calvin's teaching on the immortality of the soul and joined Luther, Tyndale and others in declaring that the dead will stay dead until they are resurrected by Christ. According to Calvin himself, "The Anabaptists in general say that souls, being departed from the body, cease to live until the day of resurrection." [33]

The Anabaptists were willing to question from Scripture any established church tradition, and on other issues differed sharply from both Lutherans and Calvinists. As a result, they were hated by both groups. History shows that Calvin and his followers succeeded in linking Luther's view of "Christian mortalism" with that of the despised Anabaptists, and popular opinion rejected it. [34]

Thus, while rejecting the Roman Catholic doctrine of purgatory, Protestantism generally failed to reject its belief that at death souls passed at once to heaven or hell. The resurrection remained an afterthought. Though Calvin rested his ultimate hope of eternal life upon Christ, it was he who put the Protestant stamp of approval on the traditional understanding of souls and their immediate reward or punishment. His influence may still be seen today.

In Calvin's monumental *Institutes of the Christian Religion*, there is a lengthy discussion of the immortality of the soul, and he

---

[32] Ibid., pp. 73 and 74.

[33] John Calvin, *Treatises Against the Anabaptists* (Baker Book House, Grand Rapids, Michigan, 1982), p. 119.

[34] Norman T. Burns, *Christian Mortalism From Tyndale To Milton* (Harvard University Press, Cambridge, Massachusetts, 1972), pp. 31-33.

commends Plato as "not only enjoyable, but also profitable" as a teacher in this area of learning. [35] One would think the following was written by an ancient Greek, but it leaked from Calvin's Platonic pen:

> The body, which decays, weighs down the soul, and confining it within an earthly habitation, greatly limits its perceptions. If the body is the prison of the soul, if the earthly habitation is a kind of fetters, what is the state of the soul when set free from this prison, when loosed from these fetters? Is it not restored to itself, and as it were made complete, so that we may truly say, that all which it gains is so much lost to the body? ... For then the soul, having shaken off all kinds of pollution, is truly spiritual, so that it consents to the will of God, and is no longer subjected to the tyranny of the flesh; thus dwelling in tranquility, with all its thoughts fixed on God. [36]

To put it mildly, one would be hard pressed to document the above statements from the pages of Scripture. To take Calvin's "logic" a step further is to conclude that the resurrection is, for the soul, a return to prison. Of greater concern is Calvin's contention that, contrary to Isaiah's prophecy, Christ did not "pour out his soul unto death." He wrote:

> Now, O dreamy sleepers, commune with your own hearts, and consider how Christ died. Did He sleep when He was working for your salvation? Not thus does he say of himself, "...as the Father hath life in himself; so hath he given to the Son to have life in himself." (John 5:26) How could he who has life in himself lose it? [37]

---

[35] Gatch, *Death: Meaning and Mortality*, p. 118.

[36] Fudge, *The Fire That Consumes*, p. 453.

[37] John Calvin, *Tracts and Treatises in Defense of the Reformed Faith* (Vol. III) (William B. Eerdmans Publishing Co., Grand Rapids, Michigan, 1958), p. 436.

In John 5: 26, Jesus employs the well known Hebrew figure of speech called "the prophetic perfect," whereby what is literally future is figuratively referred to in the past tense. The context of John 5:20-30 is clearly regarding the future, after the resurrection and exaltation of Jesus Christ by which He will receive from God "...life in himself." It is He Who will then give everlasting life to those who have believed on Him, and judge all men.

Apparently Calvin did not believe that Jesus actually died. To say that Christ did not truly die means that He was not truly resurrected and thus could not be the Savior of man.

1 Corinthians 15:3 and 4

(3) For I delivered unto you first of all that which I also received, how that Christ died for our sins according to the scriptures,

(4) And that he was buried, and that he rose again the third day according to the scriptures:

Christ was not "working for our salvation" after He died, but while He was *alive,* being "...obedient unto death, even the death of the cross" (Philippians 2:8). The implications of Calvin's enormous error are vast. It was his Augustinian theology that drowned out Luther, Tyndale and others and guided the doctrinal outcome of the Reformation.

In the Spring 1990 issue of *Resurrection Magazine*, Norman Raxworthy wrote:

Why has this glorious (and practical) truth of the resurrection become so diffused and neglected in the Church today? The reasons for this situation go back into history. In the third century, Christian apologists sought to defend Christianity within the framework of Greek philosophy. Origen (d. 254), for example, freely adopted Platonic thought as a means of explaining Christian doctrine. To the Jews it was argued that Christ was the fulfillment of prophecy, and a Christian understanding of the Hebrew Scriptures was developed. To the Greeks, however, the argument was that Christianity was not only consonant with Greek philosophy, but was perhaps the very culmination of it. Thus the Hellenists were able to accept a Christianity that taught soul-survival as the hope of the believer, rather than resurrection (an idea repugnant to much of Greek thought). So Paul was reconciled to Plato. As a modern scholar comments: "Not surprisingly the Greek view of the soul had infected the early church, whose catch-phrase was '*soma-sema*' ('the body a tomb'). To their minds the soul was released from its prison at death."

There are Christians today who still see resurrection in this kind of way, and think that "rising from the dead" means that at death their soul ascends to heaven. But this idea is not taught in the Scriptures. Indeed, the very reason why the Greeks of Paul's day could not accept the resurrection was that they believed in the immortality of the soul. The idea of resurrection is at odds with the doctrine of the immortality of the soul. [38]

You Shall Be As Gods

In contrast to Plato, who believed that a man's soul is *eternal* and thus existed before the body it inhabited, orthodox Christian writers through the years have generally qualified their teaching that man has an immortal soul. Most have said that each man's immortality had its beginning as a gift from God.

W.G.T. Shedd is representative of the traditional understanding of man's innate immortality.

> But irrepressible and universal as it is, the doctrine of man's immortality is an astonishing one, and difficult to entertain. For it means that every frail finite man is to be as long-enduring as the infinite and eternal God; that there will no more be an end to the existence of the man who died today than there will be for the Deity who made him. God is denominated 'The Ancient of Days.' But every immortal spirit that ever dwelt in a human body will also be an 'ancient of days.' ...Yes, man must exist. He has no option. Necessity is laid upon him. He cannot extinguish himself. He cannot cease to be. [39]

---

[38] Norman Raxworthy, "Resurrection: The Christian Hope," *Resurrection Magazine* (Spring 1990), pp. 8 and 9.

[39] W.G.T. Shedd, *The Doctrine of Endless Punishment* (Charles Scribner's Sons, New York, 1886), p. 490.

Such doctrine is in effect little different than Satan's original hand-in-hand lies: "...ye shall be as gods..." and "...Ye shall not surely die." Thus the original lie of the soul's immortality is still being advanced today, with multiple and horrendous ramifications. It strikes at the heart of Christian doctrine regarding the nature of man and the impossibility of his redemption apart from God's grace. Edward John Carnell eloquently helps us separate truth from error in this regard:

> Instead of teaching that man is of such infinitely incontestable value, that God, to be worthy of His name, must preserve him immortally, the Christian follows Paul's judgment that there is none righteous, no not one (Romans 3:10). Man, then, deserves *death*, not life. The Christian cannot appeal to the rationality of the universe, for all rationality is from God. He cannot claim an independent rule of goodness and justice to assure him of life, for all goodness and justice flow from God.
>
> In short, the Christian knows that man, a vile, wretched, filthy sinner, will receive immortal life solely and only by God's grace; man neither deserves immortality nor is worthy of it. Unless He that made man sovereignly elects to give him salvation and life, by grace and not by works, man is absolutely without hope. [40]

The Christian's hope is not an immortal soul, but the appearing of the Lord Jesus Christ, when those believers who are alive will be instantly caught up and given new bodies. At the same time, those who have fallen asleep will be awakened to everlasting life.

---

[40] Edward John Carnell, *An Introduction to Christian Apologetics* (William B. Eerdmans Publishing Co., Grand Rapids, Michigan, 1948), pp. 344 and 345.

CHAPTER THREE

What Is Death?

Dead or Not Dead?

"Dead." The word has a sickening finality to it. This is especially true when you first hear it used to describe someone integral to your life whom you love fervently. There is a terribly frustrating hopelessness about the terminal state of death, and in many cases an anguished survivor has grabbed and shaken a dear friend who has just died, saying something like, "Don't do this to me."

Man's hopelessness about death has in large part been responsible for the proliferation of theories and fables regarding an immediate "life after death" for everyone. Each of these is nothing more than an attempt to deny the horrifying reality of death. This denial of death fits with man's inherent desire for instant gratification, which is no doubt more prevalent in our materialistic western culture. Popular language about death attempts to camouflage its monstrous reality. Euphemistic terms such as "passed away," or "deceased" are good examples. As we will see, God's choice of the metaphor of one "falling asleep" maintains the truth about death while taking away some of its sting.

Since one's body and soul are inseparable in life, it would follow that the same holds true in death. In any language, "death" is the absence of life that once was. In the biblical languages and in English usage, death has both a literal and a figurative meaning. Let us look first at the literal meaning. Quite rightly, English dictionaries define "death" and "dead" in terms of "life" and "living": "having ceased to live" (*Funk and Wagnall*) or "deprived of life" (*Webster*). The mutually exclusive nature of these two terms is biblically apparent also.

Deuteronomy 30:19

I call heaven and earth to record this day against you, *that* I have set before you life and death, blessing and cursing: therefore choose life, that both thou and thy seed may live:

Luke 24:5

And as they were afraid, and bowed down *their* faces to the earth, they said unto them, Why seek ye the living among the dead?

1 John 5:12

He that hath the Son hath life; *and* he that hath not the Son of God hath not life.

On the literal level of meaning, both in biblical languages and in English, a living being is either still "living" or it is "dead" (not living). "Death" is the ending of "life." When something has ceased to "live," it is "dead." If it is "dead," then it is not "living." It cannot be "dead" and "not dead" at the same time and in the same literal sense. This is elementary logic, upon which depends the value of language as a tool for communication of truth.

A brief look at how the New Testament juxtaposes the two Greek words *zoe* (life) and *thanatos* (death) makes clear their antithesis. The following verse is a good example:

Romans 6:23

For the wages of sin *is* death [*thanatos*]; but the gift of God *is* eternal life [*zoe*] through Jesus Christ our Lord.

If we cannot depend on the language of the Bible, we cannot be sure that God's Word reveals truth about the state of the dead or any other subject. To remain logical and consistent with the entire thrust of Scripture, we must conclude that biblically, one who is "dead" is *truly* dead and not "alive" in any sense of the term.

As stated, the Hebraic understanding of the human being was that his body and soul were totally integrated and neither could exist without the other. Considering an apple seed may help us understand this inseparable union. So integrated is its life with its body that, if one could isolate the life that it contains, the seed and the life in it would be destroyed.

Only when language is used figuratively is it possible for a living thing to be dead physically, but alive in some other manner. This is true both in the biblical languages and in English. Such figurative usages of "dead" are found in Romans 6:2 and Ephesians 2:1, where Christians are said to be "dead" to sin, that is, they are alive in Christ, via the holy spirit He has given each one. It should be noted, however, that even in figurative usage, the mutually exclusive definitions of "dead" and "alive" are maintained.

Prior to their salvation, the Ephesian believers had been physically alive, but spiritually "dead" in sin. This usage of "dead" pertains to the spiritual death that was the penalty for Adam's sin.

Romans 5:12

Wherefore, as by one man [Adam] sin entered into the world, and death by sin; and so death passed upon all men, for that all have sinned:

"Soul," or physical life, pertains to literal, physical death, and "holy spirit," or everlasting life, pertains to the figurative usage of death. In the absence of soul, the body is truly and literally dead (Genesis 2:7). In the absence of holy spirit, the person is figuratively, or spiritually, dead (1 John 5:12; Ephesians 2:1 and 5).

Incidentally, some have argued that the Greek language forces the conclusion that a Christian is *presently* in possession of "eternal life."[41]

---

[41] Martin, op. cit., *Kingdom of the Cults,* p. 387.

They somewhat disparagingly refer to the idea that a Christian's future bodily death necessitates his future bodily resurrection as "conditional immortality." Their position is that one who has "eternal life" cannot truly die, for even if the physical body dies, the "eternal life" lives on.

Such a position shows a lack of understanding of the Greek word *aionios*, which appears 71 times in the New Testament, and which is always translated either "eternal" or "everlasting." This word does convey the idea of one living forever, but there is much more to it than that.

Old Testament verses such as Daniel 12:2; Job 19:25-27, et al. made it clear that "eternal life" would be attained only by way of *resurrection*, and that resurrection would eventually lead to new life in what the Bible calls "Paradise." This is the biblical "New Age." By the time of Jesus, the "everlasting life" spoken of by Daniel had come to mean life in the future age prophesied throughout Scripture.

Thus, as used in the New Testament, the word *aionios* ("of the age") refers to life in the age to come, as contrasted to "...the present evil age..." (Galatians 1:4-NIV). This fact is well documented by Christian scholars such as Alan Richardson.

> What appears in the English versions of the Bible as 'eternal life' or 'life everlasting' really means 'the life of the age to come.'...Throughout the New Testament 'eternal life' means the 'life of the age to come.' It is synonymous with the kingdom of God. Thus, in the discussion about the conditions of entry into the reign of God, the rich man in Mark 10:17 asks: '...Good Master, what shall I do that I may inherit eternal life?' Or again, if we examine the parallelism of Mark 9:43-47, we shall see that to enter 'life' and to enter the kingdom of God are one and the same thing... The chief implication of 'aeonian life' ('eternal life') is not eternal or everlasting life, but *life pertaining to the age to come.* [42]

---

[42] Alan Richardson, *Introduction to the Theology of the New Testament* (SCM Press, Ltd., London, 1958), pp. 73, 74 and 108.

In his well-known and highly respected *Lexicon of The New Testament,* Joseph H. Thayer addresses the same issue.

> As the Jews distinguished 'this age,' the time before the
> Messiah, and the 'coming age,' the time after the advent of the
> Messiah, so most of the New Testament writers distinguish 'this
> age' (or simply 'the present age'—Matthew 13:22; Mark 4:19;
> Galatians 1:4; 1 Timothy 6:17; 2 Timothy 4:10; Titus 2:12), the
> time *before* the appointed return or truly Messianic advent of
> Christ...and the *future* age (or 'that age'—Luke 20:35), 'the
> coming age' (Luke 18:30; Matthew 12:32), i.e., the age *after* the
> return of Christ in majesty, the period of the establishment of
> the Divine Kingdom with all its blessings. [43]

As Christians, we have the "earnest," or downpayment, on our promised life in the age to come, which is the gift of holy spirit we received from the Lord Jesus Christ at the moment of our new birth. We will receive the whole purchased possession at Christ's coming (2 Corinthians 1:22; 5:5; Ephesians 1:10-14). Making the downpayment into a literally present possession in full to substantiate the continuity of consciousness of the dead does great damage to biblical integrity.

Either we now have the guarantee of life in the age to come and still must contend with the literal reality of death, or we now literally have everlasting life, in which case death becomes figurative. The orthodox position makes death figurative except for the literal death of the body, which is relatively insignificant since the essential person lives on. A study of Scripture renders this position completely invalid.

Speaking about the normal meaning of death, Henry Constable wrote:

> This old sense, first stamped on it by God himself, in the
> opening period of human history, has also been the universal
> idea formed of it wherever man has lived and died. It is always

---

the primary—and in the case of the great majority of humankind, the only—meaning of the word, in every language and every tribe of the earth. "The world," says Athenagoras, "regard death as a deep sleep and forgetfulness."

This primary sense of the word has been strongly impressed on the human mind by the perpetual recurrence of death itself among all the creatures. As a result, even though numberless words in the progress of time have assumed senses wholly alien or contrary to their original meaning, this word "death" has remained true to its original in its various applications. Thus we have in Scripture the expressions "dead to sin" and "dead to the law."

And in ordinary life we speak of persons being "dead" to certain passions or affections. All such expressions are derived from physical death, and are true to its original sense. They imply the departure and consequent non-existence of relations and feelings which were once living and strong—*their death*. Sin has ceased to be dear to the renewed mind: the old relation of the law has ceased to be for the believer: the former friend no longer lives. In every case, something has disappeared from existence. [44]

What Does The Old Testament Say?

Most orthodox writers contend that the Old Testament has little to say about what happens after death, but this is hardly the case, as we shall see. In answering the question "What is death?" we must consider foundational verses in the Old Testament that establish the idea that the dead are truly dead and not conscious or alive in any sense of the word. In doing so, we must remember a simple principle regarding biblical study: Unless there is some clear shift between the Old and the New Testaments that would lead us to a new awareness of truth in regard to

---

[44] Henry Constable, *The Duration and Nature of Future Punishment* (Excerpts from his book, first published in 1868, were in an article entitled "The Old Testament and Sin's Penalty" in *Resurrection* Magazine, Vol. 94, #4, Fall 1991), p. 9.

a particular subject, we ought to preserve the traditions of the Old Testament revelation as being also "the Word of God."

The Old Testament is "the New Testament concealed," and we need the New Testament revelation to guide us in interpreting it on many points. However, Romans 15:4 says that the Old Testament is "...for our learning,..." and we ought not to assume that every doctrine it declares will be overturned in the New Testament. Our continual quest in biblical study is to propound truth consistent with the Bible as a whole. We must not select texts that develop a micro-position inconsistent with the macro-position of the entire Bible.

Such is certainly the case with the subject of the state of the dead. Squeezing a theological position out of a few particular verses while overlooking larger scriptural themes and clear verses on the subject is at best poor scholarship and at worst dishonest. Furthermore, it is critical that we be sensitive to the original Hebraic stamp on the entire Bible and realize how much the later extraneous influence of Greek philosophy and language contributed to historic "Christian" theology.

The Psalms are a particularly fruitful place to begin our study of the Old Testament. What they say regarding the state of the dead ought to be regarded as authoritative.

Psalm 49:12 and 14

(12) Nevertheless man *being* in honour abideth not: he is like the beasts *that* perish.

(14) Like sheep they are laid in the grave; death shall feed on them; and the upright shall have dominion over them in the morning; and their beauty shall consume in the grave from their dwelling.

Psalm 89:48

What man *is he that* liveth, and shall not see death? Shall he deliver his soul from the hand of the grave? Selah.

nephesh

In these verses, we see that death is universal and overpowering. No man can deliver his own soul from the grave, which is its (the soul's) destination. "The hand of the grave" refers to the power of the grave. [45] Only God's power is greater than the grave's.

From the Old Testament, we learn also that there is no consciousness in the grave:

Psalm 6:5

For in death *there is* no remembrance of thee: In the grave who shall give thee thanks?

Psalm 30:9

What profit *is there* in my blood, when I go down to the pit? Shall the dust praise thee? shall it declare thy truth?

Psalm 88:11 and 12

(11) Shall thy lovingkindness be declared in the grave? *or* thy faithfulness in destruction?

(12) Shall thy wonders be known in the dark? And thy righteousness in the land of forgetfulness?

Psalm 115:17

The dead praise not the LORD, neither any that go down into silence.

Psalm 146:4

His breath goeth forth, he returneth to his earth; in that very day his thoughts perish.

---

[45] E.W. Bullinger, *The Companion Bible* (Samuel Bagster and Sons Limited, London, England, 1964), p. 808.

Isaiah 38:18

> For the grave cannot praise thee, death can *not* celebrate thee:
> they that go down into the pit cannot hope for thy truth.

So in death there is only silence, with no remembrance, no thoughts, no praise, no hope, no celebration. No thanks! In a very significant Old and New Testament metaphor, which we will later analyze in depth, this condition of unconsciousness is called "sleep."

Job 14:12

> So man lieth down, and riseth not: till the heavens *be* no more,
> they shall not awake, nor be raised out of their sleep.

A consistent biblical theme is the parallel comparison of death to sleep. Some argue that the sleep metaphor is used primarily in the New Testament and refers only to the body sleeping and never to the soul or the whole person. [46] This is patently false. The Hebraic conception of death is that of "sleep," from which God delivers and redeems people through the vehicle of resurrection.

In the Bible, *the body is requisite to life* and therefore must be restored in order for the soul, the whole person, to be revived. There is no biblical indication that a disembodied "soul" or "spirit" lives on after a person is dead.

Job 7:21

> And why dost thou [God] not pardon my transgression, and take
> away mine iniquity? for now shall I sleep in the dust; and thou
> shalt seek me in the morning, but I *shall* not *be*.

---

[46] Martin, op. cit., *The Kingdom of the Cults*, p. 389.

If Job believed that his soul would go to heaven when he died, he would not have said, "You [God] will search for me, but I will be no more." Job would be "no more" because he would be dead and awaiting the resurrection necessary for him to be alive again.

Consider the following verses in regard to both the concepts of sleep and a future resurrection:

Daniel 12:2

And many of them that sleep in the dust of the earth shall awake, some to everlasting life, and some to shame and everlasting contempt.

Psalm 49:15

nephesh

But God will redeem my soul from the power of the grave; for he shall receive me. Selah.
includes
nephesh physical body + instincts
→ neph = physical body + instincts

Notice that his "soul," not just his body, is *in the grave*. Biblically, the "soul," as previously noted, refers to his whole being, which is in the grave. Does a Christian need to fear the grave? No! Why? Because God will redeem his whole being from the grave. What great words of comfort to those who believe. Other references to the grave and resurrection, such as the following, occur in Job.

Job 14:13 and 14

(13) O that thou wouldest hide me in the grave, that thou wouldest keep me secret, until thy wrath be past, that thou wouldest appoint me a set time, and remember me!

(14) If a man die, shall he live *again*? all the days of my appointed time will I wait, till my change come.

Because of the tragedy that befell him, Job was despondent—so despondent that he wished to die. Yet he realized that death would only keep him from his present pain, not bring him into a state of heavenly bliss. That, he knew, was dependent upon God "remembering" him and one day raising him from the dead with a new body. Job knew the chan would come in God's appointed time and that, until then, he woulu remain in the darkness of the grave. This is clear in the following verses:

Job 10:20-22

(20) *Are* not my days few: cease *then, and* let me alone, that I may take comfort a little,

(21) Before I go *whence* I shall not return, *even* to the land of darkness and the shadow of death;

(22) A land of darkness, as darkness *itself; and* of the shadow of death, without any order, and *where* the light *is* as darkness.

If he had been expecting to go to heaven, Job would hardly have described it as "a land of darkness." Finally, consider both the doctrinal and practical clarity of these verses:

Ecclesiastes 9:4-6 and 10

(4) For to him that is joined to all the living there is hope: for a living dog is better than a dead lion.

(5) For the living know that they shall die: **but the dead know not any thing**, neither have they any more a reward; for the memory of them is forgotten.

(6) Also their love, and their hatred, and their envy, is now perished; **neither have they any more a portion for ever in any** *thing* **that is done under the sun.**

(10) Whatsoever thy hand findeth to do, do *it* with thy might; for *there is* **no work, nor device, nor knowledge, nor wisdom, in the grave**, whither thou goest.

What happens to the body at death? There can be no argument here. Genesis 3:19 says "...for dust thou *art*, and unto dust thou shalt return." In the Old Testament culture, a dead body was buried in the ground, and this burial spot was a *qeber,* or "grave." But whether the body is buried in the ground, dumped in the ocean or cremated, it eventually is recycled by nature to the point that it no longer exists except in the memory of God. Nevertheless, our hope of everlasting life is secure. God will remember and bring to life all those who have believed His Word.

CHAPTER FOUR

Where Are the Dead?

A Grave Question

Orthodox Christian teaching is that at death the soul departs to one of two literal places, "heaven" or "hell." But this doctrine does not account for those believers who died prior to the resurrection of Jesus Christ. We believe Charles F. Baker's work entitled *Dispensational Theology* is representative of its confusion. In a chapter entitled "The Intermediate State: The Place of the Dead," in the section "*Sheol-Hades*," Baker writes:

> It would **appear** that as far as the unsaved are concerned there has been no change in their state since the death of the first one. There **seems** to have been a change brought about by the resurrection of Christ which affects the state of the saved dead, but whether this is a change of actual location or a matter of more complete revelation is **not clear**. Of one thing we may be sure: the saved dead are now with the Lord awaiting resurrection. [47] (Emphasis ours).

---

[47] Baker, op. cit., *Dispensational Theology*, p. 579.

Can we really be "sure" when things are "not clear"? Such confusion is due to men making *literal* that which is *figurative* in the Bible.

What happens to the "soul" at the death of the body? In Scripture, the soul figuratively "departs." Genesis 35:18a shows this figurative usage. "And it came to pass, as her soul [*nephesh*=life] was departing, (for she died)...." To where does the soul "depart"? It "departs" to *sheol*, which is often translated "hell," but which biblically means the grave, or "gravedom." [For a thorough examination of the meaning of the Old Testament Hebrew word *sheol* and the corresponding New Testament Greek word *hades*, the reader is referred to the word "hell" in E.W. Bullinger's *A Critical Lexicon and Concordance to the English and Greek New Testament* (Zondervan Publishing Co., Grand Rapids, Michigan).]

The following verses show two things: first, that at death the soul departs to *sheol*, and second, that the believer's hope of deliverance from the grave by resurrection is secure.

Psalm 16:10

For thou wilt not leave my soul in hell [*sheol*—gravedom];
neither wilt thou suffer thine Holy One to see corruption

Psalm 49:15

But God will redeem my soul from the power of the grave
[*sheol*— gravedom]: for he shall receive me. Selah.

It is significant that in Psalm 49:15 the Hebrew word for "receive" is *laqach*, which means "to take away." God, through Christ, will "take away" the dead from the grave.

In Greek mythology, Hades was the god of the underworld, and his name came to represent this fictitious place. The Septuagint was a second-century B.C. Greek translation of the Old Testament, and in it the word *hades* was chosen as the counterpart to the Hebrew *sheol*. As they do with *sheol*, many English versions of the Bible erroneously translate the Greek word *hades* as "hell" rather than "grave."

In his lexicon, Dr. E.W. Bullinger makes a thorough case for the translation of both *sheol* and *hades* as "gravedom," a word he apparently coined to describe "the state of being of the dead" in the most biblically accurate manner. This state—*the* grave—is different than *qeber*—a grave, because *sheol* exists only as a concept, not an actual place. Bodies buried in a *qeber*, a literal grave, will eventually disappear. *Sheol* is the figurative state, or "dwelling place," of the dead.

Though some who champion the traditional doctrine of immediate life after death have argued that *sheol* was a literal place of eternal torment, Scripture plainly says otherwise. *The Interpreter's Dictionary of the Bible* states: "Nowhere in the Old Testament is the abode of the dead regarded as a place of punishment or torment. The concept of an infernal "hell" developed in Israel only during the Hellenistic period..." [48] Edward Fudge quotes *Baker's Dictionary of Theology*: "*Sheol* is uniformly depicted in the Old Testament as the eternal amoral abode of both righteous and unrighteous alike." [49]

A figure of speech is a legitimate grammatical construction designed to emphasize a particular point. A figure of speech arrests our attention by its departure from literal fact or normal grammatical usage. Thus to recognize a figure of speech, we must first identify the literal truth regarding the subject.

Because *sheol* means "gravedom", where there is no consciousness, Scripture references referring to those in *sheol* walking, talking, etc., must be figurative. For example:

Isaiah 14:8-10

(8) Yea, the fir trees rejoice at thee, *and* the cedars of Lebanon, *saying*, Since thou art laid down, no feller [woodcutter] is come up against us.

(9) Hell from beneath is moved for thee to meet *thee* at thy coming: it stirreth up the dead for thee, *even* all the chief ones of the earth; it hath raised up from their thrones all the kings of the nations.

---

[48] *Interpreter's Dictionary of the Bible* Vol. 1(Abington Press, New York and Nashville, 1962), p. 788.

[49] Fudge, op. cit., *Fire That Consumes*, pp. 81 and 82.

(10) All they shall speak and say unto thee, Art thou also
become weak as we? art thou become like unto us?

The context of these verses is the fall of the king of Babylon (verse
4). His fall would have made the fir trees and cedars in Lebanon
"rejoice," because they were prized for lumber and often carried off to
Babylon (verse 8). Via the figure of speech personification, the trees are
vividly portrayed as rejoicing because no one has come to cut them
down. Verse nine continues this figurative language, as the dead
welcome their new companion.

When the Bible says that Jesus descended into "...the lower parts
of the earth" (Ephesians 4:9), it means that He died and was buried in
hades, or "gravedom." In Hebrews 2:9, God's Word says about Jesus
"...that he by the grace of God should taste death for every man." For
three days and three nights, Jesus was as dead as anyone else who ever
tasted death. As Isaiah plainly stated regarding the death of the Messiah:
"...he was cut off out of the land of the living..." (53:8); "...he made his
grave with the wicked . . . in his death..." (53:9).

It is too bad that *sheol* and *hades* have been translated into the
English word "hell," which has today taken on the mythological Greek
meanings associated with the pagan idea of an "underworld" where the
dead continue to live on in torment. E.W. Bullinger's comments on the
word *hades* in Appendix 131 of *The Companion Bible* are extremely
enlightening:

The meaning which the Greeks put upon it does not concern us;
nor have we anything to do with the imaginations of the
heathen, or the traditions of Jews or Romanists, or the teachings
of demons or evil spirits, or of any who still cling to them.

The Holy Spirit has used it as one of the "words pertaining to
the earth," and in so doing has "purified" it, "...*as* silver tried in a
furnace..." (Psalm 12:6). From this we learn that His own words
"are pure" but words belonging to this earth have to be "
purified."

The Old Testament is the fountain-head of the Hebrew
language. It has no literature behind it. But the case is entirely
different with the Greek language. The Hebrew *Sheol* is a word
Divine in its origin and usage. The Greek *Hades* is human in its

origin and comes down to us laden with centuries of development, in which it has acquired new senses, meanings, and usages.

Seeing that the Holy Spirit has used it in Acts 2:27 and 31 as His own equivalent of *Sheol* in Psalm 16:10, He has settled, once for all, the sense in which we are to understand it. The meaning He has given to *Sheol* in Psalm 16:10 is the one meaning we are to give it wherever it occurs in the New Testament, whether we transliterate it or translate it. We have no liberty to do otherwise, and must discard everything outside the Word of God.

A Matter of Life or Death

Another corollary doctrine of pagan origin is promulgated along with the idea that the "dead" are "alive." If man is "deathless," there must be an everlasting dwelling place for the evil as well as the good. Thus arose the concept of "hell" as a place of eternal torture for all sinners, who supposedly go there immediately upon death.

"Hell" was a grossly erroneous word to choose for the meaning of *hades*. Despite the fact that today people are constantly being told to go there, *there is no such place!*

As we have seen, however, *sheol/hades* (gravedom) is a figurative "place." The dead "exist" only in the mind of God, who remembers every person who has died. He will send His Son, "...the firstborn from the dead..." (Colossians 1:18; Revelation 1:5), to raise the rest of the dead from this "place" (John 5:28 and 29).

There is a place of "...everlasting destruction from the presence of the Lord..." (2 Thessalonians 1:9) mentioned in the Bible. This is *gehenna*, which refers to the fire of judgment in which the wicked will one day be consumed.

Gehenna is the Greek word for the Hebrew "valley of Hinnom," which was the city dump outside of Jerusalem. It was common knowledge to the people Christ was addressing that garbage was thrown into "gehenna" to be burned up. No one listening to Christ teach believed that the garbage continued to exist in the fire without being consumed. The point of Jesus using the word "gehenna" was to clearly show that those who were not saved were like the garbage, to be burned up and destroyed.

Gehenna is also called "the lake of fire" in the Book of Revelation. It is the place where fire will bring to pass the ultimate annihilation of the Devil and his hosts. Ezekiel 28:18 foretold this destruction by fire that would bring Satan "to ashes." Apparently, as a fitting recompense for his monstrous evil, this will take quite a while. According to Revelation 20:10, "forever and ever" is better translated "unto the ages of the ages." [50]

All people who have "done evil" will also one day be destroyed in this lake of fire. Why? Because the wages of sin is *death*—not eternal torment. Thus Jesus Christ died in place of sinners to pay the legal penalty for the sin of all men. In *The Fire That Consumes*, Edward Fudge quotes James D.G. Dunn in his essay, "Paul's Understanding of the Death of Jesus:"

> Had there been a way for fallen man to overcome his fallenness ... Christ would not have died ... But Christ, Man, died because there is no other way for man—any man. His death is an acknowledgement that there is no way out for fallen men except through death—no answer to sinful flesh except its destruction in death. [51]

In the same context, Fudge quotes Oscar Cullmann's *Immortality of the Soul or Resurrection of the Dead? The Witness of the New Testament*, that Jesus:

> ... can conquer death only by actually dying, by betaking Himself to the sphere of death, the destroyer of life, to the sphere of 'nothingness,' of abandonment by God ... Whoever wants to conquer death must die; he must really cease to live— not simply live on as an immortal soul, but die in body and soul,

---

[50] E.W. Bullinger, *A Critical Lexicon and Concordance to the English and Greek New Testament* (Tenth Edition) (Samuel Bagster and Sons Limited, London, England, 1971), page 259.

[51] Fudge, op. cit., *Fire That Consumes*, p. 229.

lose life itself, the most precious good which God has given us ... Furthermore, if life is to issue out of so genuine a death as this, a new divine act of creation is necessary. And this act of creation calls back to life not just a part of the man, but the whole man—all that God had created and death had annihilated. [52]

For those who believe in Jesus Christ, He has paid the price for their sin and given them the gift of life in the age to come. Those who do not believe in Him will pay the penalty for sin *themselves*. How? By dying twice, once in this life and once and for all in the lake of fire, which is referred to as the "second death" (Revelation 20:6 and 14). Everlasting life is just that—life without end—and everlasting death is destruction without hope of recall—permanent extermination. This is God's perfect justice, and it is definitely "a matter of life or death."

John 5:28 and 29

(28) Marvel not at this: for the hour is coming, in the which all that are in the graves shall hear his voice,

(29) And shall come forth; they that have done good, unto the resurrection of life; and they that have done evil, unto the resurrection of damnation [judgment].

Revelation 20:15

And whosoever was not found written in the book of life was cast into the lake of fire.

Scripture gives no hint that, when the unjust are raised from the dead for final judgment, they will be raised with new, immortal bodies as will be the case with just people. When human bodies are put into a crematorium, which is usually about 1700 degrees, they burn up. It is only a guess, but it seems likely that the "lake of fire" will be somewhat hotter than any man-made fire. Considering that one day "... the elements shall melt with fervent heat, the earth also and the works that are therein shall

---

[52] Ibid., p. 230.

be burned up" (2 Peter 3:10), it seems logical that human bodies will follow suit.

In the Bible, the purpose of fire is to purge the bad from the good by burning it up.

Matthew 3:12

Whose fan *is* in his hand, and he will throughly purge his floor, and gather his wheat into the garner; but he will **burn up** [*katakaio*—to consume] the chaff with unquenchable fire.

This word *katakaio* is used in Hebrews 13:11 regarding the sacrificial beasts that were burned outside the camp. Neither chaff nor beasts burn forever. They burn up and are gone. Many verses make this clear, such as the one that follows:

Malachi 4:1

For, behold, the day cometh, that shall burn as an oven; and all the proud, yea, and all that do wickedly, shall be stubble; and the day that cometh shall burn them up, saith the LORD of hosts, that it shall leave them neither root nor branch.

Nowhere does the Word of God say that He will torment forever those who have refused to believe in Him. Among other things, this would be irreconcilable with Revelation 21:4, which states that from then on throughout eternity there will be no more sorrow, crying or pain.

Sidney Hatch well expresses how farfetched is the idea of a just God forever tormenting by fire those who refused to believe in Him.

A civilized society looks with horror upon the abuse and torture of children or adults. Even where capital punishment is practiced, the aim is to implement it as mercifully as possible. Are we to believe then that a holy God—our heavenly Father— is less just than the courts of men? Of course not. [53]

---

[53] Sidney A. Hatch, "The Terrible Doctrine of Eternal Torment," *Brief Bible Studies* (July-December 1990), p. 17.

And with regard to this same subject, the late Swedish Lutheran Bishop John Persone wrote:

> . . . For me it is inexplainable how a person, who holds the orthodox view [of final punishment], can at any time have a glad moment in this life. He is constantly mingling with people whose final destiny will be to be tormented eternally without end. . . To me it is even more inexplainable that such an 'orthodox' person can expect even a happy moment in eternity, when he knows that contemporaneously with his blessed estate, continue the endless torment and agony of innumerable millions of the accursed. Can he, if he loves his neighbors as himself, yes, even if he has just a little bit of human love and is not solely a selfish wretch, have even a single happy moment? [54]

Another word, *tartaros,* is used once and translated "hell" in 2 Peter 2:4. It refers to the place of imprisoned evil spirits, rather than a place of torment for sinners.

Two verses in Proverbs are pertinent to this issue and help to make clear the truth that those who refuse to believe God's Word have no hope of everlasting life under any conditions.

Proverbs 24:19 and 20 (NIV)

(19) Do not fret because of evil men or be envious of the wicked,

(20) for the evil man has no future hope, and the lamp of the wicked will be snuffed out.

For a superb biblical exposition of the subject of everlasting death versus everlasting torment, the reader is referred to *The Fire That Consumes*, by Edward Fudge (available through Christian Eductional Services, Inc.). Writing in the Fall 1990 issue of *Resurrection Magazine*, Fudge summarized some of the main points of his book as follows:

---

[54] "Pastoral Letter," 1910, 21,24 and 25, cited in Froom, *The Conditionalist Faith of Our Fathers*, Vol 2 (Washington, D.C.: Review and Herald, 1965), p. 769.

1. The Old Testament utilizes some 50 Hebrew verbs and 75 figures of speech to describe the ultimate end of the wicked—and every one sounds exactly like total extinction.

2. The notion of unending conscious torment arose for the first time in anything resembling biblical literature in the noncanonical book of Judith—in a clear "twisting" of words taken straight from Isaiah.

3. By Jesus' day, there were at least three "Jewish" ideas about the end of the wicked: (a) annihilation at the grave; (b) resurrection for everlasting torture; and (c) resurrection for judgment followed by total and irreversible extinction in hell.

4. When our Lord taught on this subject, he generally used Old Testament language which most naturally describes complete disintegration of the entire person in the fire of the Age to Come.

5. New Testament writers choose the word "hell" (*gehenna*) to describe the fate of the lost *only* in the Gospels, *only* speaking to Jews, and *only* when addressing people familiar with the geography of Jerusalem.

6. Most often, New Testament authors use the words *die, death, destroy, destruction, perish* and *corruption* to describe the end of the wicked—in contexts which suggest the normal, straight-forward meaning of these ordinary terms.

7. All New Testament expressions thought to teach eternal torment come from earlier biblical literature—where they regularly describe destruction that is irresistible, total, and which cannot be reversed.

8. No passage of Scripture teaches the inherent or natural immortality of the "soul" or of any other aspect of the human creature.

9. Although Scripture clearly affirms a resurrection of both just and unjust, the Bible nowhere says the *lost* will be raised *immortal*, as the saved will be.

10. The notion of everlasting torment appears explicitly in Christian literature for the first time in the writings of the Apologists, who expressly base it on the Platonic assumption that the soul is "immortal" and *cannot* be destroyed. [55]

---

[55] Edward Fudge, "A Loving Challenge to The Evangelical Church," *Resurrection Magazine* (Fall 1990), p. 4.

In Robert H. Mounce's work, "The Book of Revelation," in *The New International Commentary on the New Testament,* his quote of Alford's statement about "the second death" is appropriate to close this chapter.

> Alford writes, "As there is a second and higher life, so there is also a second and deeper death. And as after that life there is no more death (Revelation 21:4), so after that death there is no more life." [56]

---

[56] Robert H. Mounce, "The Book of Revelation," *The New International Commentary on the New Testament* (William B. Eerdmans Publishing Co., F.F. Bruce, General Editor), p. 367.

CHAPTER FIVE

In What State of Being Are the Dead?

The "Sleep" Metaphor

1 Thessalonians 4:13

But I would not have you to be ignorant, brethren, concerning them which are **asleep**, that ye sorrow not, even as others which have no hope.

As we have seen, the dead are truly dead and in "gravedom." When their bodies have rotted, they have ceased to exist. But because they "exist" in the memory of God, He remembers them and intends via Jesus Christ to raise them to life. Thus He figuratively refers to their state of being as "sleep." This clearly implies a future awakening. Because both their body and soul are dead, the term "sleep" has to be a metaphor.

The purpose of biblical figures of speech is to communicate truth more effectively or forcefully than would simple statements of fact. A metaphor or analogy is useful to augment our understanding if we carefully analyze the points of similarity between the compared terms. In this case, death and sleep have at least five points of similarity that give us much insight into the state of the dead, consistent with what we have already seen from the Old Testament.

The first similarity between death and sleep is that both are overpowering forces. A human being needs to rest. If deprived of sleep long enough, a person will literally fall asleep in the midst of any task, no matter how demanding. The human will is no match for the power of sleep. Consider Jesus' disciples. Close to the time when He would be arrested, Jesus and His disciples were on the mount of Olives. There was probably no more critical time for Peter and the disciples to stay awake and pray.

Mark 14:35-38

(35) And he went forward a little, and fell on the ground, and prayed that, if it were possible, the hour might pass from him.

(36) And he said, Abba, Father, all things *are* possible unto thee; take away this cup from me: nevertheless not what I will, but what thou wilt.

(37) And he cometh, and findeth them sleeping, and saith unto Peter, Simon, sleepest thou? couldest not thou watch one hour?

(38) Watch ye and pray, lest ye enter into temptation. The spirit truly *is* ready, but the flesh *is* weak.

Like sleep, death is an inexorable force for all men (unless they are still living when Christ appears). No amount of self-discipline can cheat "The Grim Reaper." The most we can ask is to be "old and full of days," as God's Word describes many Old Testament saints upon whom He had conferred His blessing. Our days on earth may be healthy and full of joy, but they will eventually end. Only when the day arrives that we receive a body fashioned like Jesus Christ's glorious body will we become immortal beings who cannot die.

A second point of similarity between sleep and death is that in either state there is no consciousness of time or space. Remember that Ecclesiastes told us that the dead "know not anything." This is also true of those who sleep, and that is why people are very vulnerable to danger while they sleep. Because we are somewhat helpless in this state, God has provided us with encouragement and a promise of protection.

Psalms 121:2-4

(2) My help *cometh* from the LORD, which made heaven and earth.

(3) He will not suffer thy foot to be moved: he that keepeth thee will not slumber,

(4) Behold, he that keepeth Israel shall neither slumber nor sleep.

Psalms 3:5

I laid me down and slept; I awaked; for the LORD sustained me.

The lack of consciousness in sleep is also illustrated in Elijah's mocking of the 450 prophets of Baal. After they had tried many times to evoke his power, saying, "...O Baal, hear us...," the Scriptures teach that there was "...no voice, nor any that answered...."

1 Kings 18:27

And it came to pass at noon, that Elijah mocked them, and said, Cry aloud: for he *is* a god; either he is talking, or he is pursuing [out for a walk], or he is in a journey, *or* peradventure he sleepeth, and must be awaked.

The analogy of waking the dead from sleep makes no sense if the dead are already conscious in a higher sphere of existence, and the argument that only the body "sleeps" in death, while the soul continues to function, holds no water. On the contrary, the sleep metaphor emphasizes the absence of consciousness.

During physical sleep, bodily functions continue uninterrupted. It is the mind that sleep reduces to un-consciousness. The following biblical usages of physical "sleep" show the mental emphasis of this concept.

1 Thessalonians 5:6 and 7

(6) Therefore let us not sleep, as *do* others; but let us watch and be sober.

(7) For they that sleep sleep in the night; and they that be drunken are drunken in the night.

The sleep metaphor thus must refer to the absence of mental awareness or consciousness, which is the major qualitative difference between the sleep state and the waking state. The sleeper is not aware of elapsed time, nor of the reality of space and time in the conditions that surround him. When he awakens, his mind becomes alert and aware once more. Likewise for one who has died, when he is raised from the dead. A dead believer is absolutely unaware of the passage of time. Whether he has been dead a few days or thousands of years, the moment of his falling asleep will be, in his conscious awareness, the moment of his awakening to new life.

A third point of similarity is that both in death and in sleep no productive work can be done. Perhaps that is why God contrasts sleep and productivity.

Proverbs 6:6-11

(6) Go to the ant, thou sluggard; consider her ways, and be wise:

(7) Which having no guide, overseer, or ruler,

(8) Provideth her meat in the summer, *And* gathereth her food in the harvest.

(9) How long wilt thou sleep, O sluggard? when wilt thou arise out of thy sleep?

(10) *Yet* a little sleep, a little slumber, A little folding of the hands to sleep:

(11) So shall thy poverty come as one that travelleth, and thy want as an armed man.

The time to work for God is while one is alive (Ecclesiastes 9:4-6 and 10). That is why God's Word states:

Psalm 116:15

Precious in the sight of the LORD *is* the death of his saints.

A saint who has died cannot work for God. Some misconstrue this verse to say that God considers the deaths of His people "valuable" to Him, because He needs them "home" with Him in heaven for some higher task. However, the word "precious," *yakar*, is better translated "costly." *Yakar* also occurs elsewhere in the context of the death of God's people, and its meaning is clearly defined.

Psalm 72:13 and 14

(13) He shall spare the poor and needy, and shall save the souls of the needy.

(14) He shall redeem their soul from deceit and violence: and precious [*yakar*] shall their blood be in his sight.

Clearly God is not saying that the death of the poor and needy is something valuable, but rather *yakar* refers to the high value to God of those who love Him. For them to die would be costly to Him. So it is with "...his saints" in Psalm 116:15. Their death is "precious" in the same sense that *The American Heritage Dictionary* defines "precious": "costly; implies especially high quality or rarity of an object; implies uniqueness and irreplaceability." The death of His saints is "precious" because those whom God has sanctified for His purposes are (1) rare, (2) unique, (3) of high quality and (4) irreplaceable. Therefore, their deaths are costly. The dead cannot work for God, so it costs Him a lot to lose one of His faithful.

Understanding this point offsets the following argument: If death is like sleep and in the *consciousness* of a Christian the moment of his death is, in effect, the moment he meets the Lord, that is no different than his going to heaven the moment he dies, and thus it provides him no more incentive to live.

On the contrary, the believer who knows that death renders him unable to enjoy fellowship with the Lord or to do anything for Him realizes not only that there is no benefit to death, but also that it causes irreparable loss to himself, his family and friends and to God.

The dead are "asleep" and thus unproductive. They no longer exist and therefore are not to be prayed for or prayed to. They are not "up there" smiling down on us, watching over us or directing us in life, in spite of what one may read, hear about or experience.

Nor are they intervening on our behalf. In a recent championship basketball game, a player, whose father had died only hours earlier, made a spectacular shot. Later in an interview, another player remarked about the shot and said that his teammate's father "put that one in." The man's father, we are to understand, was apparently hovering over the basket and helping his son sink difficult shots. An obvious question arises: Did not the other team have any deceased relatives who could have blocked the shot?

In an article in *USA Today,* a woman who won two $250,000 keno jackpots said it was her dead father who inspired her to play at a specific club. She said that her father stood at the foot of her bed one night, comforting her about her money problems. "Baby," she recalls him telling her, "stop worrying. Everything's going to be okay."[57]

God's Word makes it plain that her "help" did not come from either her human father or from her heavenly Father, but rather from the "father of lies." There *is* an abundance of heavenly help available, however, from God the Father, His Son Jesus Christ and millions of angels. We are much better off relying on all this divine power than looking to dear Aunt Ethel, who, as "dust," is currently helpless.

A fourth point of similarity is that sleep takes place in a limited time period, sandwiched between one's falling asleep and waking up.

Mark 4:27

And [the sower] should sleep, and rise night and day, and the seed should spring and grow up, he knoweth not how.

---

[57] "Reno Winner Has Father's Smarts," *USA Today* (September 27, 1990).

The phrase "sleep and rise night and day" illustrates a continuance of rising and sleeping for a period of days. Thus we can see that each state of sleep has a beginning and an end. Similarly, for a Christian, death is not final. It is an interim state that ends in an awakening.

A fifth similarity between death and sleep is that there is a continuity of being of the person when he awakens from sleep. The same person falls asleep and awakens again. Peter was still Peter after he awoke in the garden. Jesus was still Jesus when He awoke from the dead and arose from the tomb.

If at death one's physical body eventually goes back to dust and thus his soul no longer exists, what then is the "continuity" factor? According to Job 14:13, a dead believer "exists" only in the memory of God, but certainly God, through Christ, is able to make a new body for him. After all, God started "from scratch" once before, didn't He?

How Did Jesus Christ Describe the State of the Dead?

To consider what Jesus said about death, we now investigate the Gospels. There is nothing in Jesus' teachings that would lend credence to the Greek concept of the immortality of the soul or the soul's survival after the death of the body. (Matthew 10:28; 22:23-32; Luke 16:19-31; 23:42 and 43; John 11:20-27; 14:2 and 3 are discussed later in this book in the chapter entitled "Difficult Scriptures Explained").

In Matthew 9:24, Mark 5:39 and Luke 8:54, Jesus also referred to the dead as "sleeping," just as the Old Testament did. The same holds true for the following verses from the record of Jesus raising his friend Lazarus from the dead. They speak for themselves regarding the sleep metaphor.

John 11:11-14

(11) These things said he: and after that he saith unto them, Our friend Lazarus sleepeth; but I go, that I may awake him out of sleep.

[handwritten marginalia: why were they if this is Jesus as they were familiar w/ death as sleep?]

(12) Then said His disciples, Lord, if he sleep, he shall do well.

(13) (Howbeit Jesus spake of his death: but they thought that he had spoken of taking of rest in sleep.)

(14) Then said Jesus unto them plainly, Lazarus is dead.

We know that Jesus Himself expected to die and be buried in the grave for three days and three nights.

Matthew 12:40

For as Jonas was three days and three nights in the whale's belly; so shall the Son of man be three days and three nights in the heart of the earth.

If the dead go to heaven to be in God's presence when they die, why wouldn't Jesus? If anyone should have been given that privilege by God, it was Jesus. He made no such claim, however, for Himself or for others.

Jesus did, however, often make mention of the resurrection of the dead, consistent with Hebrew understanding. For example:

Luke 14:14

And thou shalt be blessed; for they cannot recompense thee: for thou shalt be recompensed **at the resurrection of the just** [not "when you die"].

Speaking of her brother Lazarus who had died four days earlier, Martha spoke to Jesus.

John 11:24-26

(24) Martha saith unto him [Jesus], I know that he [Lazarus] shall rise again in the resurrection at the last day.

(25) Jesus said unto her, I am the resurrection, and the life: he that believeth in me, though he were dead, yet shall he live:

(26) And whosoever liveth and believeth in me shall never die....

Note that neither Jesus nor Martha spoke of Lazarus as if he were alive in heaven. Lazarus, raised by Jesus after being dead for four days, was not rudely yanked out of heaven where he was revelling in celestial bliss. Rather, he was restored to life.

Where had Jesus learned about resurrection, specifically His own? From the Scriptures. Jesus had studied the Old Testament and knew therefore that He was to be raised from the dead. The record of Isaac's figurative resurrection (compare Genesis 22:1-18 to Hebrews 11:17-19) was a type of his own literal resurrection, and scriptures such as these bolstered Jesus' faith in God's promise. Perhaps the two most notable Old Testament verses regarding the Messiah's resurrection are Psalms 2:7 and 16:10. These also were etched upon Jesus' heart.

Psalm 2:7

I will declare the decree: the LORD hath said unto me, Thou *art* my Son; this day have I begotten thee.

In hindsight, we recognize that this is a reference to His *resurrection*, not His birth, as we shall see shortly when we consider what Paul said in Acts 13.

In all the Old Testament, Psalm 16:10 is perhaps the most specific verse referring to the raising of the Messiah from "gravedom."

Psalm 16:10

For thou wilt not leave my soul in hell [*sheol*=gravedom]; neither wilt thou suffer thine Holy One to see corruption.

After His resurrection, Jesus Christ taught His disciples these and other Old Testament verses that enabled them to understand the significance of His death and resurrection (Luke 24:27 and 45; Acts 1:3). Peter in particular elevated the importance of Psalm 16:10 by quoting it twice in his discourse on the day of Pentecost.

What Did Peter Say?

Not long after Jesus had taught His disciples Psalm 16:10, this signal verse became the main point of Peter's sermon on the day of Pentecost:

Acts 2:22a and 24

(22a) Ye men of Israel, hear these words; Jesus of Nazareth...

(24) Whom God hath raised up, having loosed the pains of death, because it was not possible that he should be holden of it.

Since the wages of sin is death and Jesus paid the price for all men's sin, He was temporarily gripped by the "pains of death." But once Jesus had died, the legally required penalty had been paid, and God could raise up His Son.

Acts 2:25-28

(25) For David speaketh concerning him [Peter then quotes Psalm 16:8-11]. I foresaw the Lord always before my face, for he is on my right hand, that I should not be moved:

(26) Therefore did my heart rejoice, and my tongue was glad; moreover also my flesh shall rest in hope:

(27) Because thou wilt not leave my soul in hell [*hades*=gravedom], neither wilt thou suffer thine Holy One to see corruption.

(28) Thou hast made known to me the ways of life; thou shalt make me full of joy with thy countenance.

[handwritten annotation]

By revelation, David had plainly said that his soul would remain in the grave unless the Messiah retrieved it. Again, Acts 2:27 (referring to Psalm 16:10) reveals that God would allow the Messiah to go to the grave, but would not allow Him to remain there to see corruption.

Peter then goes on to make a statement that is perfectly consistent with what has already been shown to be the thrust of Scripture, that the dead are truly dead and sleeping in "gravedom."

Acts 2:29

Men *and* brethren, let me freely speak [i.e., speak frankly] unto you of the patriarch David, that he is both dead and buried, and his sepulchre is with us unto this day.

No mention is made of David inhabiting the "great beyond" and looking down on the events of Pentecost with a smile. In fact, Peter is making a clear statement that, in contrast to Jesus Christ being raised from the dead, David is still dead. Unless the dead are really dead, the resurrection from the dead loses its great significance and the most important event in the history of mankind, namely Christ's resurrection, is rendered virtually meaningless.

In Acts 2:31, Peter repeats Psalm 16:10, rewording it in terms of it having been accomplished: "He seeing this before, spake of the resurrection of Christ, that his soul was not left in hell, neither his flesh did see corruption." By quoting it again, Peter identified it as the focal verse of the context. Verse 34 further establishes the contrast between David, who penned the words of Psalm 16:10, and Jesus Christ, who lived them.

Acts 2:34 and 35

(34) For David is not ascended into the heavens: but he saith himself, The Lord said unto my Lord, Sit thou on my right hand,

(35) Until I make thy foes thy footstool.

Could it be any plainer? David did not go to heaven when he died. And he is not in a holding pattern above Chicago. David understood that, when he died, he would stay dead until God exalted the Messiah to His right hand and then sent Him to raise David to life in the age to come. Peter also understood this truth.

What About Paul?

Paul's great discourse in Acts 13:16-41 contains the same truths as Peter's preaching on Pentecost. The two most significant apostles of the first-century church agreed on the state of the dead and on the resurrection of the dead.

Acts 13:32 and 33

(32) And we declare unto you glad tidings, how that the promise which was made unto the fathers,

(33) God hath fulfilled the same unto us their children, in that he hath raised up Jesus again; as it is also written in the second psalm, Thou art my Son, this day have I begotten thee.

Paul's reference is to Psalm 2:7b, and he leaves no doubt that the resurrection of Jesus Christ fulfilled this promise.

Acts 13:34-37

(34) And as concerning that he raised him up from the dead, *now* no more to return to corruption, he said on this wise, I will give you the sure mercies of David.

(35) Wherefore he saith also in another *psalm*, Thou shalt not suffer thine Holy One to see corruption:

(36) For David, after he had served his own generation by the will of God, fell on sleep, and was laid unto his fathers, and saw corruption.

(37) But he, whom God raised again, saw not corruption.

As did Peter at Pentecost, Paul also quoted Psalm 16:10. His terminology is the same on every point. David died, saw corruption (returned to dust) in the grave and is now "asleep" and awaiting resurrection. The phrase "slept with his fathers" is a common Hebrew expression for death, often used in the Old Testament. Paul's use of a similar expression in Acts 13:36 further supports the complete agreement of both Old and New Testaments regarding the state of the dead and supporting the idea of resurrection—a future awakening.

When Paul wrote abut the recovery of Epaphroditus, who had been deathly ill, he said that "...God had mercy on him [Epaphroditus]..." (Phil. 2:27). Would it be mercy to deprive someone of "heaven?" No, it was *mercy* for God to heal him. For a believer, long life on earth is always portrayed as a blessing from God, not a postponement of glory.

Rest In Peace

In light of the sleep metaphor, it is clear that death is certainly not something to be desired or eagerly anticipated. It remains the mortal enemy of life and godliness, both of which can only be enjoyed by the living. It robs God of our love, worship and service. It robs us of our fellowship with God and the joy of living. Yet one who is born again need not fear what will happen to him while he is dead, for death is simply an interim state of "unconsciousness" to be ended by the coming of Jesus Christ. Christians asleep in death are unconscious of time, and hence their next waking moment is the coming of Christ. Christians who have died may, as the saying goes, "rest in peace."

Before we end our discussion of the sleep metaphor, it will be interesting to allow Martin Luther to speak on the subject. Though his words are in no way equal to God's Word, they are set forth here to remind the reader to the fact that this book's authors are among many in history to have recognized this vital truth in God's Word. It is too bad that Luther did not more vigorously include in his Reformation theology the truth that he obviously believed at one time.

The following quotes by Luther are taken from an article entitled "What Happens To People When They Die?" written by Blaine Newman in the Winter 1990 issue of *Resurrection Magazine*. (Sources are footnoted for the reader's information.)

> It would take a foolish soul to desire its body when it was already in heaven. [58]
>
> For just as a man who falls asleep and sleeps soundly until morning does not know what has happened to him when he wakes up, so we shall suddenly rise on the last Day, and we shall know neither what death has been like nor how we have come through it. [59]
>
> Another proof that the dead are insensible. Solomon thinks, therefore, that the dead are altogether asleep, and think nothing. They lie, not reckoning days or years, but, when awakened, will seem to themselves to have slept scarcely a moment. [60]
>
> We Christians, who have been redeemed from all this through the precious blood of God's Son, should train and accustom ourselves in faith to despise death, and regard it as a deep, strong, sweet sleep; to consider the coffin as nothing other than a soft couch of ease or rest. As verily, before God, it truly is just this; for he testifies, John 11:21(sic. proper reference is John 11:11): Lazarus, our friend sleeps; Matthew 9:24: The maiden is not dead, she sleeps. [61]
>
> For since we call it a sleep, we know that we shall not remain in it, but be awakened and live, and that the time during which we sleep, shall seem no longer than if we had just fallen asleep. Hence, we shall censure ourselves that we were surprised or alarmed at such a sleep in the hour of death, and suddenly come alive out of the grave and from decomposition, and entirely well, fresh, with a pure, clear, glorified life, meet our Lord and Saviour Jesus Christ in the clouds ... [62]

---

[58] Paul Althaus, translated by Robert C. Schultz, *The Theology of Martin Luther* (Fortress, Philadelphia, 1966), p. 417.

[59] Ibid., p. 414.

[60] Froom, op. cit., *Conditionalist Faith* (Vol. 2), p. 77.

[61] Ibid., p. 77.

[62] Ibid., p. 78.

Just as soon as your eyes are closed you will be awakened. A thousand years will seem as though you have slept a half an hour. As we do not know how long we are sleeping if we do not hear the clock striking during the night, so in death a thousand years will pass away still more rapidly. [63]

We are to sleep until he comes and knocks on the grave and says, "Dr. Martin, get up." Then I will arise in a moment and will be eternally happy with him.

Did You See Elvis?

What about accounts of so-called "near-death" or "post-death" experiences, which have perhaps become more in vogue in recent years due to the improvement in medical technology? After being revived, some people have described either glorious or hideous visions and/or conversations with God, Jesus, the Devil, angels, dead relatives or friends. It is not surprising that among doctors, theologians, amateur philosophers and Hollywood producers there are many explanations for these stories.

First of all, no explanation that contradicts God's Word can be valid. Obviously we cannot rule out God giving someone a vision even when he is near death, but if one were in fact clinically dead, it is clear from Scripture that no one could communicate with him.

At least some doctors agree. Dr. John Caronna, professor of clinical neurology at New York Hospital-Cornell Medical Center in New York City, referring to those who have "essentially died and been resuscitated," said, "As a physician and a neurologist, I believe that this period is totally blank and that even if something happened during that period, it would not be remembered." [64] Any "firsthand" reports to the contrary must be satanic counterfeits designed to promote his original lie, "...Ye shall not surely die."

---

[63] Althaus, *op. cit.,Theology of Martin Luther*, p. 17.

[64] Wendy Benedetto, "Near-Death Experiences Are Likely Dreams," *USA Today* (Wednesday, January 2,1991), p. 9a.

Scripture records a number of instances when people were raised from the dead by Jesus and other men utilizing the power of God. Such miracles obviously blessed the families and friends of the ones who were raised to life. Were these living people selfishly desiring their dead loved ones to leave Paradise and rejoin them in this cruel world? No. And it is *most* significant that not one of those raised from the dead professed any experiential knowledge of an afterlife.

In conclusion, the dead are in a state of "sleep." The sleep metaphor simply and profoundly answers the question, "In what state of being are the dead?" In His wisdom, God has achieved an artful balance, preserving the idea of death as an enemy, but robbing death of its "sting," so that we as Christians with the blessed hope of our Savior's appearing and the guarantee of everlasting life need not sorrow "...even as others which have no hope" (1 Thessalonians 4:13).

CHAPTER SIX

When Will the State of "Sleep" End?

What a Body!

Thus far we have seen that the dead are truly dead and are "sleeping" in "gravedom." It is interesting that the English word "cemetery" comes from the Greek word *koimeterion*, the verb root of which means "to put to sleep." It is the word often used in the New Testament for the "sleep" of death.

In the case of a person who has been buried at sea, we say he has a "watery grave." In a relatively short amount of time, his body occupies no "place" at all. This holds true for everyone who has died. The molecules of matter that made up his body are recycled into other organisms, plants or sediments. One's life, however, is not recycled. Figuratively speaking, the person "sleeps" in "gravedom," or "hell," the state of the dead. In this state, he "exists" only in the mind of God, who remembers every person who has ever lived (Job 14:13). One's body, soul and everything about him is recorded in God's memory. Accordingly, God has given Jesus Christ the power to call all people back to life (John 5:25-30).

Remember that to the Greeks who believed in the dualism of one's physical body and his immortal soul, a resurrection of the body was superfluous. We can clearly see this by a comment made by those in Athens in response to Paul's preaching of Jesus Christ and resurrection.

Acts17:18

Then certain philosophers of the Epicureans, and of the Stoicks,
encountered him. And some said, What will this babbler say?
other some, He seemeth to be a setter forth of strange gods:
because he preached unto them Jesus, and the resurrection.

In contrast to that of the Greeks, the Hebrew conception of life
after death necessitated one having a body. This is the proper scriptural
perspective. To the Hebrews, the body and soul were inseparable
realities, neither being able to exist without the other. If a person (a soul)
was to be revived, he had to have a body, for no life can exist without
a body. This is certainly the evidence of nature. Every living thing on
earth has a body (1 Corinthians 15:38-40). The life of every species of
organism is perpetuated only by reproduction, with each generation
being made in the genetic form of its predecessors. As Genesis 1:11, 12,
21, 24 and 25 expresses it, everything reproduces "after his [its] kind."
    The life of an individual organism dies when the organism dies. Its
life is not recycled into another organism of its own or another species.
This is important to understand because there is a move afoot in the New
Age "scientific" community to change the biological life cycle. Instead
of birth-reproduction-death, some now teach that the cycle is birth-
death-rebirth. It is being claimed that not only matter, but also the life
that animates it, is reborn into new organisms. This is nothing but
reincarnation in a white lab coat.
    The Old Testament teaching on resurrection was that a person
would be resurrected with essentially the same body he had when he was
previously alive.

Job 19:26 and 27 (NIV)

(26) And after my skin has been destroyed, yet in my flesh I will
see God;

(27) I myself will see him with my own eyes—I, and not another.
How my heart yearns within me!

The New Testament expands upon this understanding and reveals that a Christian's body will be changed into a glorious new body, made like Jesus Christ's resurrected body.

1 John 3:2

Beloved, now are we the sons of God, and it doth not yet appear what we shall be: but we know that, when he shall appear, **we shall be like him**; for we shall see him as he is.

There is no reason to suppose that this body will be much different in form than its original version. The differences will be in its quality of life, its scope of activity and its immortality. One would assume that the genetic uniqueness of each individual will be preserved, without the effects of disease, age or sin.

Incorruptible Seed

Some may be concerned that, if in death their body and soul cease to exist, there is no "continuity factor" of their person. According to the traditional view, there is a continuity of consciousness via the "immortality of the soul". The extinction of one's being, even temporarily, is hard to accept. All believers can take comfort in knowing that God's memory of dead believers is perfect and reliable. At the resurrection, each believer will still be himself or herself. No one will be wondering who he was in this life. There is another element of continuity for the Christian, which is the gift of holy spirit, as 1 Corinthians Chapter Fifteen explains.

In Corinth, there were "some" (1 Corinthians 15:12) among the Greek Christians who held to the pagan doctrine of the immortality of the soul, saying that there is no resurrection of the body. The Word of God goes to considerable length to show that a bodily resurrection is necessary and, for Christians, guaranteed.

1 Corinthians 15:17 and 18

(17) And if Christ be not raised, your faith *is* vain; ye are yet in your sins.

(18) Then they also which are fallen asleep in Christ **are perished**.

If Christ is not alive and able to raise the dead, then those who have died believing in Him are "perished." Why? Because they are *not* alive in heaven in any form. They are dead in the grave, and only the resurrected Lord Jesus Christ can give them life. Thus, any teaching that Old Testament believers were alive in heaven prior to Christ's resurrection is bogus.

Furthermore, if Jesus Christ has not been raised from the dead, then one who believes on Him as Lord is not even saved, because His resurrection is prerequisite to His Lordship. The formula for salvation is simple.

Romans 10:9 and 10

(9) That if thou shalt confess with thy mouth the Lord Jesus, and shalt believe in thine heart that God hath raised Him from the dead, thou shalt be saved.

(10) For with the heart man believeth unto righteousness; and with the mouth confession is made unto salvation.

The thrust of 1 Corinthians Chapter Fifteen is that Jesus Christ was raised from the dead, and therefore He will, in the future, raise all who have believed on Him. Until that time, they are dead. As He was raised bodily, so will He raise others to everlasting life by giving them immortal bodies. The point is that *human beings* need *bodies* to have *life*. As the present temporal animating life force of one's physical body is his soul, so the future animating life force of one's spiritual body in the age to come will be holy spirit.

1 Corinthians 15:35

> But some *man* will say, "How are the dead raised up? and with
> what body do they come?"

That is a very good question and one that deserves a godly answer.

1 Corinthians 15:36-38

> (36) *Thou* fool, that which thou sowest is not quickened, except
> it die:
>
> (37) And that which thou sowest, thou sowest not that body
> that shall be, but bare grain, it may chance of wheat, or of some
> other *grain*;
>
> (38) But God giveth it a body as it hath pleased him, and to
> every seed his [its] own body.

In mankind, physical birth is the result of a physical seed being
"planted" by a man in a woman. (It is interesting that the Greek word for
"seed" is *sperma*.) Spiritual birth also involves a seed.

1 Peter 1:23

> Being born again, not of corruptible seed, but of incorruptible,
> by the word of God, which liveth and abideth for ever.

This verse speaks of the new birth any person can receive by
adhering to Romans 10:9. The word "seed" is figurative, because the
holy spirit nature one acquires when he is "born again" is intangible.
Why does God call this gift of life "seed"? Because it is what the Bible
calls an "earnest" (2 Corinthians 1:22; 5:5; Ephesians 1:14), that is, a
token or downpayment on what is to come. Therefore, if a Christian is
"planted" in death, this incorruptible "seed" will one day blossom into
an incorruptible "body" after its kind. God's gift of holy spirit is the
"continuity" factor.

1 Corinthians 15:42-44

(42) So also *is* the resurrection of the dead. It is sown in corruption; it is raised in incorruption.

(43) It is sown in dishonour; it is raised in glory: it is sown in weakness; it is raised in power:

(44) It is sown a natural body; it is raised a spiritual body. There is a natural body, and there is a spiritual body.

Customarily, if one wants apples, one plants an apple *seed*, not an apple itself. An apple seed, if planted, will one day have an apple "body." It is worth noting that the apple "body" is much more attractive and useful than the apple seed that was planted. So it is with a human being. "Seed" implies *birth*. A corruptible, natural, human seed (sperm) results in one's "natural" (physical) bodily birth. The incorruptible spiritual "seed" of holy spirit (1 Peter 1:23; 1 John 3:9) that each Christian receives when he is born again will result in his new "spiritual body" when Jesus Christ appears.

In verses 51ff, 1 Corinthians 15 goes on to give more details about the destiny of those who during their lifetime receive the "seed" of holy spirit.

1 Corinthians 15:51-54

(51) Behold, I shew you a mystery; We shall not all sleep, but we shall all be changed,

(52) In a moment, in the twinkling of an eye, at the last trump: for the trumpet shall sound, and the dead shall be raised incorruptible, and we [living Christians] shall be changed.

(53) For this corruptible [dead Christians] must put on incorruption, and this mortal [living Christians] *must* put on immortality.

(54) So **when** this corruptible shall have put on incorruption, and this mortal shall have put on immortality, **then** [and only then] shall be brought to pass the saying that is written, Death is swallowed up in victory.

Note that death is not swallowed up in victory until Christ comes. If Old Testament believers or Christians went immediately to heaven when they died, then death, not resurrection, would be the victory.

The Prince of Life

Much has already been said about the significance of Jesus Christ's resurrection, but we will review. If the dead are truly dead and "sleeping" in "gravedom," and no one has ever gotten up from the dead except to live out his natural life on earth (e.g., Lazarus), then the stage is set for appreciating the uniqueness and importance of Jesus' bodily resurrection. In this light, the entire New Testament clearly shows how much depends on the incredibly significant act of God raising His Son from the dead.

The first reference in the Bible to Jesus Christ is in Genesis 3:15, where He is figuratively called a "seed." Why did God choose that term? Because after His suffering, death, resurrection, ascension and exaltation as Lord, Jesus Christ was to be given "...life in himself" (John 5:26). He is the "firstfruits" of those who have died (1 Corinthians 15:20), and He will one day produce much more fruit by generating a new race of immortal men **"after His kind."**

Jesus Christ is called the "Prince of life" (Acts 3:15). The word for "Prince" is the Greek word *archegos*, which means the first one in a column. Jesus Christ is the first man ever to conquer death. It is He Who has blazed a trail to God's heart for all men who believe on Him to follow.

Jesus is also called "...the captain [*archegos*] of their salvation..." (Hebrews 2:10). He is the "...firstborn from the dead..." (Colossians 1:18) and the "...firstborn among many brethren" (Romans 8:29). Having defeated the power of the grave, Jesus Christ will raise all the dead in the fullness of time (1 Corinthians 15:22). It is He who will bring "... many sons unto glory " (Hebrews 2:10). Were it not for God's magnificent power (Ephesians 1:19 and 20) that He gave to Christ to raise the dead, they would remain dead for eternity.

When will the dead be made alive? Jesus Himself made this clear.

John 14:2 and 3

(2) In My Father's house are many mansions: if *it were* not *so*, I would have told you. I go to prepare a place for you.

(3) And if I go and prepare a place for you, I will come again, and receive you unto Myself; that where *I* am, *there* ye may be also.

No believer will literally be given everlasting life until Jesus again appears and receives him unto Himself. The first time Jesus Christ will raise the dead is when He appears to gather together the Church, His body, in the air. As previously noted, 1 Corinthians 15:51-58 refers to this event. 1 Thessalonians 4:13-18 adds more details. The same basic truth is set forth, and we see that it is Jesus Christ Who will at His appearing awaken "sleeping" saints.

1 Thessalonians 4:13

But I would not have you to be ignorant, brethren, concerning them which are alseep, that ye sorrow not, even as others which have no hope.

When someone we love dies, God does not expect us not to sorrow. Grief is a godly process designed to enable a person to deal with such a tragedy. In this verse, we see that knowledge concerning those who have died will help us not to sorrow as do those with no hope. The knowledge is in regard to our hope, and the next verse begins to elaborate upon that hope. Knowing the truth about our hope of life in the age to come gives us a basis for true joy amidst our grief.

1 Thessalonians 4:14

For if we believe that Jesus died and rose again, even so them also which sleep in Jesus will God bring with him.

After the word "sleep," the verse is better translated "God will by means of Jesus bring with Him." [65] The context is regarding those who have died. As we have seen, they are in the dust of the earth, or "gravedom." The verse cannot be saying that Jesus will bring them with Him *from* heaven because they are not *in* heaven. Rather, by way of Jesus coming for them, God will bring them with Jesus *from* the grave *to* heaven. How? Let's keep reading.

1 Thessalonians 4:15

For this we say unto you by the word of the Lord, that we which are alive *and* remain unto the coming of the Lord shall not prevent [go before] them which are asleep.

Some Christians will live until the appearing of the Lord Jesus Christ.

1 Thessalonians 4:16

For the Lord himself shall descend from heaven with a shout, with the voice of the archangel, and with the trump of God: and the dead in Christ shall rise first:

There sure is a lot of *noise* in that verse. Why, it's enough to wake the dead. Yes, it is!!!

1 Thessalonians 4:17 and 18

(17) Then we which are alive, *and* remain shall be caught up together with them in the clouds, to meet the Lord in the air: and so shall we ever be with the Lord.

(18) Wherefore comfort one another with these words.

---

[65] Bullinger, op. cit., *The Companion Bible*, p. 1792.

Regarding 1 Thessalonians 4:13-18, Sir Anthony Buzzard shrewdly observes that in Thessalonica:

> ...the question had arisen in the minds of the believers as to what would be the state of those Christians who had died before the expected return of Jesus. Now Paul could have so easily removed all anxiety by pointing out that the dead in Christ were already with him, having at the moment of their death overcome the grave and passed to their reward in heaven. It is well known that he says nothing of the sort.

> ...he offers comfort to the believers in connection with those Christians who are said to be "sleeping", an extraordinary term to use if He thought they were already fully conscious in bliss with the Lord...In a similar situation today, the church would be consoled with claims that the dead are already alive with God. [66]

Most everyone has wondered about what happens to babies or young children who die before they reach the age when they are able to understand the Gospel message and decide for themselves whether or not they want to believe in Jesus Christ. There is only one verse we know of that seems to specifically address that issue, and it is 1 Corinthians 7:14, where the Word, speaking of children of one or both Christian parents, states that they are "holy," which means "set apart." To us that indicates that the goodness and grace of God extends beyond the lives of Christian parents to encompass any of their children until they can make their own decision about Jesus Christ. One thing we do know for certain is that God is righteous, and thus He will be fair and just to everyone, including those who live and die without ever hearing the truth of His Word.

What genuine comfort it is to know that when Jesus Christ appears to gather together all Christians, those who have died and those still alive, He will give each one a glorious new body just like his own.

---

[66] Anthony Buzzard, *What Happens When We Die?* (The Restoration Fellowship, Oregon, Illinois), pp. 38 and 42.

Philippians 3:20 and 21

(20) For our conversation [citizenship] is in heaven; from
whence also we look for the Saviour, the Lord Jesus Christ:

(21) Who shall change our vile body, that it may be fashioned
like unto his glorious body, according to the working whereby
he is able even to subdue all things unto himself.

Later, after a period of great tribulation on earth, Jesus Christ will
come with the Church *to the earth* to save Israel at Armageddon. Unlike
His first coming, when national Israel rejected Him, at His second
coming, they will hail Him as Messiah and King. It is then that Jesus
Christ will raise those people who believed God during Old Testament
times as well as all people who believed the gospel of the kingdom
during the time of tribulation. This resurrection is known both as the
"resurrection of the just" (Luke 14:14; Acts 24:15) and the "resurrection
of life" (John 5:29).

Finally, after the thousand years in which Christ reigns as King on
earth, generally known as "the Millennium," He will raise the remaining
dead for the final "white throne judgment" (Revelation 20:11-15). This
final resurrection is known both as the "resurrection of damnation
[judgment]" (John 5:29) and the "resurrection of the unjust" (Acts
24:15; 2 Peter 2:9). At that time, those who believed on Him during the
Millennium will be given everlasting life. All unbelievers of all ages
will also be resurrected at that time, and those whose names are not
found written in the book of life will be cast into the lake of fire and
destroyed forever. All those whom Jesus Christ has raised to new life
will then live forever with Him and God in the genuine biblical New Age
on the new earth that the Bible refers to as "Paradise."

Here Comes the Judge

At this point, it should be noted that, according to God's Word,
there is no judgment issuing in either reward or punishment until Jesus
Christ comes to do the judging. The traditional view of orthodoxy that
judgment (and reward or punishment) takes place immediately after

death is totally contrary to scriptural truth. Saint Peter is not presently taking tickets at the Pearly Gates. The Bible clearly refers to a specific "day of judgment" sometime in the future.

For Christians, "judgment" takes place at the gathering together of the Church, the Body of Christ. Since Jesus Christ by His death paid the penalty for sin, each Christian has been made righteous in Him. Therefore Christ's "judgment" of each Christian at this time is not in regard to whether he will have everlasting life, which is a gift already guaranteed to him, but to evaluate his works as a Christian.

Like hope, judgment is associated with the coming of Jesus Christ and not the moment of one's death. Christ is not forced to render specific judgments each time that someone dies, because this "judgment" is a future event at a specific time. Until this time of judgment, the dead remain in a "waiting" state. As we have already explained, this waiting state is called "sleep."

Consider these pertinent scriptures:

Luke 14:14

And thou shalt be blessed; for they cannot recompense thee: for thou shalt be recompensed **at the resurrection of the just**.

John 12:48

He that rejecteth me, and receiveth not my words, hath one that judgeth him: the word that I have spoken, the same shall **judge him in the last day.**

Acts 17:31

Because he hath appointed **a day**, in the which he will judge the world in righteousness by *that* man whom he hath ordained; *whereof* he hath given assurance unto all *men*, in that he hath raised him from the dead.

Romans 2:5

But after thy hardness and impenitent heart treasurest up unto thyself wrath against **the day of wrath and revelation** of righteous judgment of God;

2 Timothy 4:1

> I charge *thee* therefore before God, and the Lord Jesus Christ,
> who shall judge the quick [living] and the dead **at his appearing**
> and his kingdom:

Consider the following verses, which clearly state that all unbelievers, regardless of when they died, will be judged at the same time.

Revelation 20:12-15

> (12) And I saw the dead, small and great, stand before God; and the books were opened: and another book was opened, which is *the book* of life: and the dead were judged out of those things which were written in the books, according to their works.
>
> (13) And the sea gave up the dead which were in it; and death and hell [*hades*= the grave] delivered up the dead which were in them: and they were judged every man according to their works.
>
> (14) And death and hell [*hades*= the grave] were cast into the lake of fire. This is the second death.
>
> (15) And whosoever was not found written in the book of life was cast into the lake of fire.

Verse fourteen is further proof that "hell" [*hades*] cannot be a literal place of *eternal* torment, because it, too, will be "destroyed." As we have seen, *sheol/hades* is only a figurative place, but since *death* will be no more, the "place" of the dead will also cease to exist. Jesus Christ will one day bring to pass "the death of death," the last enemy to be destroyed.

Revelation 21:4

> And God shall wipe away all tears from their eyes; and there shall be no more death, neither sorrow, nor crying, neither shall there be any more pain: for the former things are passed away.

(For a more thorough discussion of when various groups of the dead will be made alive and a general chronological overview of eschatological ("end-times") events, the reader is referred to *Things To Come* by J. Dwight Pentecost (Zondervan Publishing Co.) and E.W. Bullinger's *Commentary On Revelation* (Kregel Publications).

Thus it is only Jesus Christ, the "last Adam," who can and will, once and for all, solve the problem of sin and death brought on by the first Adam. Because Jesus obeyed God all the way unto death, "...even the death of the cross," God has highly exalted Him (Philippians 2:8 and 9) and given Him all authority in heaven and on earth (Matthew 28:18). God has also given His Son everlasting life in Himself (John 5:26). Jesus Christ will awaken from the sleep of death all who have believed in Him, and give them life in the age to come. Thus He will put back together and bring to pass God's original plan of a family living together forever.

1 Corinthians 15:54b-58

(54b) ... then shall be brought to pass the saying that is written,
Death is swallowed up in victory.

(55) O death, where *is* thy sting? O grave, where *is* thy victory?

(56) The sting of death *is* sin; and the strength of sin *is* the law.

(57) But thanks *be* to God, which giveth us the victory through our Lord Jesus Christ.

(58) Therefore, my beloved brethren, be ye stedfast,
unmoveable, always abounding in the work of the Lord,
forasmuch as ye know that your labour is not in vain in the Lord.

This last verse is God's exhortation to all Christians, based upon our hope of everlasting life at the appearing of Jesus Christ. This hope is described in Hebrews 6:19 as an "...anchor of the soul...." Thus we can stand, steadfast and unmoveable, "...always abounding in the work of the Lord...." Our labor is not in vain.

CHAPTER SEVEN

Difficult Scriptures Explained

A vital principle of Bible interpretation that must be upheld in handling any subject in God's Word is that any verses that are harder to understand must be analyzed in light of clear verses on the same subject. "Clear" verses are not just those that agree with one's theological position. They are those that seem to be straightforward and literal statements of fact. Figurative expressions that seem to be contradictory can best be handled after the literal, factual position is determined. The Bible should be accepted literally whenever possible. When verses seem to contradict previously established facts, one is justified in exploring other possible meanings that are consistent with the whole Bible.

We have laid the solid biblical foundation that death is the total absence of life, that there is no part of a person (either "soul" or "spirit") that "goes to heaven" when he dies and that the dead are actually dead and "sleeping" in "gravedom" until Christ's appearing. We now turn our attention to some sections of Scripture commonly misconstrued to indicate otherwise. Let us remember that they must harmonize with those parts of God's Word that we have already examined.

1 Samuel 28

(The woman of Endor)

As previously noted in Chapter One, 1 Samuel 28 describes the woman of Endor conjuring up "Samuel" from the dead for King Saul. It is important to note Saul's original request: "...Seek me a woman that hath a familiar spirit...." (1 Samuel 28:7). The context, specifically verses 7-9, along with other Old Testament verses already cited, shows that she did, in fact, perform this spiritual phenomenon through "familiar spirits." These were evil spirits that manipulated her and impersonated Samuel, with whom they were "familiar."

A key to understanding this record in Chapter 28 is in verse 13.

1 Samuel 28:12 and 13

(12) And when the woman saw Samuel, she cried with a loud voice: and the woman spake to Saul, saying, Why hast thou deceived me? for thou *art* Saul.

(13) And the king said unto her, Be not afraid: for what sawest thou? And the woman said unto Saul, I saw gods ascending out of the earth.

In verse 13, the Hebrew word for "gods" is *elohim*, a word used in various ways in the Old Testament. Here it refers to an evil spirit that the woman saw, one that was impersonating Samuel. In verses 12-20, God's Word reports this incident as the participants perceived it, and refers to this spirit as "Samuel."

What "Samuel" (the familiar spirit) told Saul was not from the LORD, for 1 Samuel 28:6 says that the Lord did not answer Saul at all. Only when Saul went to a woman who dealt with familiar spirits did he get an answer, but that answer was not from God. In fact, Saul's going to the woman at Endor partly contributed to his death.

> came to pass — was true

1 Chronicles 10:13

So Saul died from his transgression which he committed against the LORD, *even* against the word of the LORD, which he kept not, and also for asking *counsel* of *one that had* a familiar spirit, to enquire *of it.*

This conjuring up of familiar spirits is the same method used today for "communicating with the dead," by which some find false and misleading comfort. The results can be as devastating as they were for Saul.

2 Kings 2:9-18

(Elijah)

2 Kings 2:11 says that Elijah "...went up by a whirlwind into heaven." This phrase in no way indicates that Elijah was taken to a place of everlasting life called "heaven." The word "heaven" has several usages in Scripture. Phrases such as "the dew of heaven," "the stars of heaven" and "the birds of heaven" all indicate a use of "heaven" that simply means the sky above the earth.

Elijah was taken from the earth into the sky by a wind; that is, he was moved from one place on earth to another. The other prophets understood this, and thus wanted to go look for Elijah. Elisha, however, knowing that God would have hidden Elijah, did not want them to look for him. 2 Kings 2:11 simply means that God supernaturally moved Elijah from one place to another, similar to what He did later with Philip in Acts.

Acts 8:39 and 40a

(39) And when they were come up out of the water, the Spirit of the Lord caught away Philip, that the eunuch saw him no more: and he went on his way rejoicing.

(40a) But Philip was found at Azotus:...

As a human being, Elijah eventually died and is awaiting the resurrection of the just.

Matthew 10:28

(Kill the body, not the soul)

Matthew 10:28

And fear not them which kill the body, but are not able to kill the soul: but rather fear him which is able to destroy both soul and body in hell [*gehenna*].

If nothing else, this verse clearly shows that the soul is *not* immortal, because it can be destroyed, but let us look at the verse more closely. The context is Jesus Christ instructing his twelve apostles before sending them out to preach the gospel of the kingdom to the lost sheep of the house of Israel (Matthew 10:5 and 6). What He tells them in verse 28 is not to fear men inspired by the Devil, who may kill them, but who can do nothing more to them after that. The following parallel passage helps us understand the above verse.

Luke 12:4 and 5

(4) And I say unto you my friends, Be not afraid of them that kill the body, and after that have no more that they can do.

(5) But I will forewarn you whom ye shall fear: Fear him, which after he hath killed hath power to cast into hell [*gehenna*]; yea, I say unto you, Fear him.

In context, verse five refers to the time of judgment of the unjust. It is God whom Jesus wanted his apostles to fear (which in essence is to respect) and to obey more than they would men who might threaten or even kill them. It is God (by way of giving Jesus Christ the authority to judge) Who will judge all men and who can also "destroy" them forever in the lake of fire.

Matthew 17:1-9

(The Mount of Transfiguration)

Matthew 17:1-9 describes a scene at what is called "the Mount of Transfiguration," where Jesus conversed with Moses and Elijah. God was preparing Jesus for the challenge of His upcoming suffering. This scene was not a literal reality, but what Jesus plainly said was a "vision."

Matthew 17:9

> And as they came down from the mountain, Jesus charged them, saying, Tell the **vision** to no man, until the Son of man be risen again from the dead.

Biblically, a vision is a spiritual phenomenon in which God causes something to appear to a person, either in his mind's eye or to his physical eyes. (Some Scriptural examples are 2 Kings 6:17; Acts 10:9-20; 2 Corinthians 12:1-4.)

Being a vision, it in no way means that Moses and Elijah made a special guest appearance from heaven where they had been hanging around since leaving earth. To be consistent with the biblical evidence, including Jesus' statement that no man but He "...hath ascended up to heaven..." (John 3:13), the same must be said of Moses and Elijah as was said of David in Acts 2:34—they are *not* "...ascended into the heavens...."

Matthew 22:23-32

(God is the God of the living)

In Matthew 22:32, Jesus said that "...God is not the God of the dead but of the living." Some teach that this verse means that there are really no dead as far as God is concerned. The text more accurately reads, "God is not the God of dead people, but of living people." As we have seen, "dead people" will become "living people" only when Jesus Christ comes to resurrect them.

In fact, the context surrounding this verse emphasizes the *resurrection* (see verses 23,28 and 30), when all shall be made alive.

Matthew 22:31 and 32

(31) But as touching the **resurrection** of the dead, have ye not read that which was spoken unto you by God, saying,

(32) I am the God of Abraham, and the God of Isaac, and the God of Jacob? God is not the God of the dead, but of the living.

God is not the God of dead people, because as Psalm 115:17 indicated, the dead cannot praise God, and Ecclesiastes 9:4-6 and 10, showed that the dead cannot do anything for Him. They are, however, still in the mind of God, and at the resurrection, they will be made living people again, and He will again be their God.

Two verses in Romans go hand-in-hand with Matthew 22:32, and also indicate that it is the Lord Jesus Christ Who will raise the dead.

Romans 14:8 and 9

(8) For whether we live, we live unto the Lord; and whether we die, we die unto the Lord: whether we live therefore, or die, we are the Lord's.

(9) For to this end Christ both died, and rose, and revived, that he might be Lord both of the dead and living.

Luke 16:19-31

(Lazarus in Abraham's bosom)

Luke 16:19-31 describes Lazarus, the beggar, after he died, as being in "Abraham's bosom." Since the Bible clearly says that in death there is no consciousness, this story must be figurative, and it is. In his book, *Are The Dead Alive Now?* Victor Paul Wierwille points out that in:

> ...two ancient Greek manuscripts—the Bezae Caulabrigiensis and the Koridethian-Caesarean text—words are included which have been deleted in other translations. Both of these ancient manuscripts begin Luke 16:19 with the words: *eipen de kai heteran parabolen,* which translated means, "And He said also another parable."[67]

Edward Fudge states that the basic plot of this parable, "the reversal of earthly fortunes after death, was familiar in popular Palestinian stories of Jesus' time."[68]

Of this section, Sir Anthony Buzzard says:

> The opening words, "Now there was a certain man...", remind us of the story of the Prodigal son and the parable of the Unjust Steward, which begin with the same phrase, and caution us that we are dealing with a story with a moral rather than a straight discourse on eschatology. "It is inconceivable," says F.W. Farrar (*Smith's Dictionary of the Bible*, Vol. 2, p. 1038) "to ground the proof of an important theological doctrine on a passage which confessedly abounds in Jewish metaphor."[69]

Verse 23 is a key to understanding it as a parable, which is a figure of speech and not literal. The verse begins "And in hell [*hades*=gravedom] he lift up his eyes ...." This makes it clear that it cannot be taken literally. In verse 24, we see that Lazarus has a tongue also. How could a disembodied "soul" have eyes and a tongue? This is more evidence that the story Jesus told was not true to fact.

---

[67] Victor Paul Wierwille, *Are the Dead Alive Now?* (American Christian Press, New Knoxville, Ohio, 1971), p. 73.

[68] Fudge, op. cit., *Fire That Consumes*, p. 203.

[69] Buzzard, op. cit., *What Happens When We Die?*, p. 51.

In context, Jesus had been addressing the Pharisees in parables from the beginning of Chapter Fifteen: the lost sheep, the lost coin, the prodigal son and the unjust steward. Luke 16:14 tells us that the Pharisees, who loved money, heard him and ridiculed him. In verse fifteen, Jesus told them that their values were warped and ungodly. The subsequent parable of the rich man and Lazarus perfectly illustrated for them the difference between what they esteemed and what God esteemed.

Not understanding this as a parable, one might think that Jesus meant to depict an immediate "heaven or hell" kind of afterlife. However, He told this parable to the Pharisees in light of their Talmudic traditions and their belief in immediate reward or punishment after death. It was they who coined the phrase "Abraham's bosom" as one of several afterlife locations. [70] Jesus did not intend to contradict the entire Old Testament and teach survival after death.

His primary intention was to show that the Pharisees were so evil that even if someone rose from the dead they wouldn't listen to him. He did so by hypothetically stating that, even if one were to return from the place of the dead (which the Pharisees, having forsaken the Old Testament in favor of their traditions, believed in), those who refused to believe Moses and the prophets *still* would not believe (verse 31). How prophetic, as was evidenced by His own resurrection from the dead, which many of them did not believe.

Of this account, *The New Bible Dictionary* says the following:

> Probably the story of Dives [according to tradition, the rich man's name] and Lazarus (Luke 16:1-9) is a parable which makes use of current Jewish thinking and is not intended to teach anything about the state of the dead. [71]

There is even more biblical evidence that this record is a parable. Remember that Revelation 21:4 states that, after all the judgments, there will be no more sorrow, crying or pain. How could saved believers

---

[70] E.W. Bullinger, op. cit., *The Companion Bible*, p. 1,484.

[71] *New Bible Dictionary*, op. cit., "Eschatology," p. 388.

possibly enjoy the riches of eternity if they were constantly being interrupted by burning people shouting up at them for water?

Luke 23:39-43

(Paradise today)

Luke 23:42 and 43 is often used to teach that the penitent malefactor who believed in Jesus immediately went to "heaven" when he died (even though the verse in question reads "paradise"). However, the phrase "I tell you the truth today" was a Hebrew idiom used to emphasize the solemnity and importance of an occasion or moment (cp. Deut. 4:26, 39 and 40; 5:1; 6:6; 7:11; Josh. 23:14). A similar kind of usage occurs in English. We often use the word "now" for emphasis even when it is not needed to communicate information. An upset parent may say to a misbehaving child, "Now you listen to me, young man." In that statement, the word "now" is not used to communicate the time, but rather used for emphasis. The same is true with the Hebrew idiom, "I tell you the truth today," which we would probably state as "Now I tell you the truth." Recognizing the Hebrew idiom and properly punctuating the verse with the comma *after* the word "today," we see that Jesus' meaning is clearly future, to be fulfilled when He comes again and establishes His kingdom on earth.

Thus the verse should read as follows: "Jesus answered him, 'I tell you the truth today, you will be with me in paradise.' "

Also, the word "paradise" is preceded by the article "the" and therefore refers biblically to the place of beauty *on earth* described in Genesis 2, lost in Genesis 3, that will be restored by the Lord Jesus Christ when He returns to earth (see Revelation 22:1-3). (For more information on "paradise," see the note on Ecclesiastes 2:5, page 908; and Appendix 173 in *The Companion Bible*, edited by E.W. Bullinger.)

Not only did the penitent malefactor not go to "paradise" that day, neither did Jesus Christ. As stated earlier, he died and spent the next three days and three nights in the grave.

John 11:20-27

("I am the resurrection and the life")

John 11 is the tremendous record of Jesus raising His friend Lazarus from the dead.

John 11:25 and 26a

(25) Jesus said unto her [Lazarus' sister Martha], I am the resurrection, and the life: he that believeth in me, though he were dead, yet shall he live:

(26a) And whosoever liveth and believeth in me shall never die...

Verse 26a is sometimes wrenched out of its context to show that no one who believes in Jesus Christ really dies. But verse 25 contains the key word to understanding verse 26: "resurrection." Jesus knew that, like all those in the Bible who were raised from the dead, Lazarus would die again. He makes it clear that in the future "he shall live." Thus whosoever lives and believes in Christ will never die *after* the resurrection.

John 14:2 and 3

(Many mansions)

John 14:2 and 3 (NIV)

(2) In my Father's house are many rooms; if it were not so, I would have told you. I am going there to prepare a place for you.

(3) And if I go and prepare a place for you, I will come back and take you to be with me that you also may be where I am.

Here Jesus told his disciples that He was going to prepare a place for them in His Father's house. Many take this promise to mean that, at death, a believer takes up residence in one of the "many mansions." Jesus made it clear in the next verse, however, that it was only when He comes back and takes them unto Him that they would be with Him.

2 Corinthians 5:1-9

(Absent from the body, present with the Lord)

2 Corinthians 5:8 is often used to teach that to be "...absent from the body..." in death is to be immediately "...present with the Lord" in heaven. However, the verse does not say that, if Paul were to die, he would *immediately* go to be with the Lord, and it can only be correctly understood in light of the context of the section of Scripture in which it is found.

In Chapter 4, verses 8-12, Paul speaks by revelation about some of the trials laid on Christians by the "...god of this age..." (verse 4-NIV), who, of course, is Satan. In verses 13-18, he cites the hope of being given everlasting life by the Lord Jesus as the unseen reality that enables a Christian to endure adversity in this life.

2 Corinthians 5:1

For we know that if our earthly house of *this* tabernacle were dissolved, we have a building of God, an house not made with hands, eternal in the heavens.

The "earthly house" is our physical body. God's Word likens it to a "tabernacle" (e.g., 2 Peter 1:13 and 14). In the Old Testament, the Tabernacle was not permanently situated. Neither is the Christian permanently situated in his earthly body. For our body to be "dissolved" means that it returns to dust at death. What is the everlasting "building of God"? It is the new body that Jesus Christ, who is presently "in the heavens," will give each Christian. *When* will this occur?

2 Corinthians 5:2

For in this we groan, earnestly desiring to be clothed upon with
our house which is from heaven:

It will occur when we are clothed upon with our house which is
from heaven. When will that be? Paul had already told the Corinthians
about this future transformation in his previous epistle (see 1 Corinthians
15:51ff). Note carefully that verse 2 does not say that one goes *to* heaven
at death. In fact, there is nothing we can do to "work" our way into God's
presence, not even by dying. Only the Lord Jesus can escort us into the
presence of God.

In the Greek text, the words "from heaven" are *ex ouranou*, which
literally mean "out of heaven," and indicate the origin of where each
Christian's new body will come from. In Luke 20:4 we see a similar
usage in regard to John's baptism. Jesus asked the chief priests if it
was "from heaven" (*ex ouranou*). In other words, He asked them if the
idea for John to baptize came from God. In the same sense, our new body
comes to us from (*ek*) God through (*dia*) Jesus Christ.

2 Corinthians 5:3

If so be that being clothed we shall not be found naked.

This means that if a Christian lives until he is "clothed upon" at the
gathering together of the Church, he will not die. Again Paul is
reiterating what he had previously written in 1 Corinthians 15:51.

2 Corinthians 5:4

For we that are in *this* tabernacle do groan, being burdened: not
for that we would be unclothed, but clothed upon, that mortality
might be swallowed up of life.

Paul specifically says here that even though the Christian life is often hard when one is involved in the battle, he does *not* want to "be unclothed," that is, die. Why? Because he knew that death was an enemy and that it would not usher him immediately into God's presence. What *did* Paul desire? To be clothed upon, while still living, with his promised "house" from heaven so "that mortality might be swallowed up by life."

2 Corinthians 5:5-7

(5) Now he that hath wrought us for the selfsame thing *is* God, who also hath given unto us the earnest of the Spirit.

(6) Therefore *we are* always confident, knowing that, whilst we are at home in the body, we are absent from the Lord:

(7) (For we walk by faith, not by sight:)

Because of the "earnest," or guarantee, of holy spirit that Christ has given us, we are always confident of His current spiritual presence with us and of our future bodily presence with Him, no matter how bad things get in this life. "Absent from the Lord" (verse 6) thus obviously refers to our not yet being *physically* present with Him in the new "house" He will give us when He appears.

2 Corinthians 5:8

We are confident, *I say*, and willing rather to be absent from the body, and to be present with the Lord.

Now verse 8 becomes very easy to understand. Paul was confident of his future life in the age to come and states that he would actually prefer to be living in that condition, that is, physically "present with the Lord" in his new body. Does the verse say that a Christian is present with the Lord at the moment of his death? No.

2 Corinthians 5:9

Wherefore we labour, that, whether present or absent, we may
be accepted of him.

Paul then says that, because of his certainty of life in the age to
come, and its rewards, he plans to give his utmost for the Lord, whether
or not he lives until His appearing.

2 Corinthians 12:1-4

(Out of the body)

2 Corinthians 12:1-4

(1) It is not expedient for me doubtless to glory. I will come to
visions and revelations of the Lord.

(2) I knew a man in Christ above fourteen years ago, (whether in
the body, I cannot tell; or whether out of the body, I cannot tell:
God knoweth;) such an one caught up to the third heaven.

(3) And I knew such a man, (whether in the body, or out ot the
body, I cannot tell: God knoweth;)

(4) How that he was caught up into paradise, and heard
unspeakable words, which it is not lawful for a man to utter.

More than a century ago, W. Laing of Edinburgh, Scotland wrote
the following regarding the above verses, and we cannot improve upon
his work:

This passage is often quoted as unanswerable evidence that a
man may see and hear without having any connection with his
body; that a man may leave his body behind him, and be taken
away to a great distance, and both see and hear in a bodiless
condition . . .

The whole weight of the argument rests on the supposition that
the terms "...in the body..." and "...out of the body..."

necessarily mean *embodied* and *disembodied*. The value of the alleged proof lies in the facts as to the usage of these terms.

The Greek word *ektos*, here rendered "out of" as in 1 Corinthians 6:18 rendered "without." Thus: "Flee fornication, every sin that a man doeth is without (*ektos*) the body; he that committeth fornication sins against his own body." Whatever meaning the Apostle attached to *ektos* here, it could not have been "disembodied." He was not referring to sins done by disembodied men. "...Every sin that a man doeth is [done] (*ektos*) without the body" (i.e., sins in general), "but he that committeth fornication sinneth against his own body."

It is not plain that the Apostle uses the words rendered, "...without the body..." in the sense of *mentally*? And if so, is it not probable that he uses the same term in the same sense in 2 Corinthians 12:2 and 3? Thus: "I knew a man in Christ, whether *mentally* or bodily I cannot tell, carried away to the third heaven, to paradise, etc." The Spirit of the Lord caught away Philip, and he was found at Azotus (Acts 8:39). Philip doubtless was caught away bodily. The Apostle John, when in the Isle of Patmos, was carried away in the Spirit "...into the wilderness..." (Rev. 17:3). The necessities of the case satisfy us that the prophet was transported mentally (like Ezekiel "in the visions of God") so that while in Pastmos he was mentally transported to the scenes described, and saw those wonderful visions of things that were to come to pass afterwards.

As vividly were the "visions and revelations" mentioned by Paul seen and heard . . . though he was unable to tell whether he was mentally or bodily present. Such, we submit, is a fair understanding of the language in question; and therefore it cannot be fairly used as indisputable proof that a man, after he is dead, is as capable of seeing and hearing as when he was alive. Proof for this improbable idea must be sought for elsewhere. [72]

---

[72] Reprinted from *The Messenger* (now *Resurrection* Magazine), April, 1888, pp. 84 and 85.

Philippians 1:21

(To die is gain)

Philippians 1:21 (NIV)

For to me, to live is Christ and to die is gain.

This verse says that "to die is gain," from which it is taught that the "gain" is going to heaven to be with God. Of course, this insidiously infers that death is not an enemy after all. It should be no surprise that once again the *context* in which this verse is set is critical to understanding it. The "furtherance," or gain, of *the gospel* is the theme of the first chapter of Philippians (see verses 17 and 27).

Philippians 1:12-14 (NIV)

(12) Now I want you to know, brothers, that what has happened to me has really served to **advance the gospel**.

(13) As a result, it has become clear throughout the whole palace guard and to everyone else that I am in chains for Christ.

(14) Because of my chains, most of the brothers in the Lord have been encouraged to speak the word of God more courageously and fearlessly.

Paul saw that his imprisonment, certainly not a personal gain, had served to further the gospel of Christ. Likewise, Paul was considering that his death, even less a personal gain, might also result in the furtherance of the gospel and in Christ being magnified.

Philippians 1:18-20 (NIV)

(18) But what does it matter? The important thing is that in every way, whether from false motives or true, Christ is preached. And because of this I rejoice. Yes, and I will continue to rejoice,

(19) for I know that through your prayers and the help given by the Spirit of Jesus Christ, what has happened to me will turn out for my deliverance.

(20) I eagerly expect and hope that I will in no way be ashamed, but will have sufficient courage so that now as always Christ will be exalted in my body, whether by life or death.

In verse 20, both life and death relate to Christ being magnified, and verse 21 reiterates the point. Paul's hope was that, whether he lived or died, the result would be gain for Christ. In verse 23, he then indicates that there is something far better than either living or dying.

Philippians 1:23 (NIV)

I am torn between the two: I desire to depart and be with Christ, which is better by far;

What was Paul's only alternative to living or dying, which was "better by far" than either of those? It was departing and being with Christ. As previously stated, Paul knew that the only time he could depart and be with Christ was when Christ appears from heaven to get him.

Putting on our new bodies and meeting the Lord in the air is far better than either living or dying. This is what every Christian, not just Paul, should eagerly anticipate as he lives for Christ now. Nowhere in this context is the idea that Paul's death would immediately bring him into the presence of Christ. 2 Timothy shows Paul's understanding of this:

2 Timothy 4:8

Henceforth there is laid up for me a crown of righteousness, which the Lord, the righteous Judge, shall give me **at that day**: and not to me only, but unto all them also that love His appearing.

It has been well said that: "If contemporary believers shared with Paul his clarity of vision and faith in the future, there would be no temptation to read into his writings the notion of a conscious pre-resurrection state." [73] Paul knew that he would receive a crown of righteousness when Jesus Christ comes to gather together His Church. This is the day we will meet him in the air "... and so [by meeting Him in the air] shall we ever be with the Lord," where He will be, first in His millenial kingdom and then on the new earth in Paradise.

Hebrews 11:5

(Enoch)

Hebrews 11:5

By faith Enoch was translated that he should not see death; and was not found, because God had translated him: for before his translation he had this testimony, that he pleased God.

First of all, verse 13 of the same chapter says "These all [including Enoch] died...." Enoch lived three generations before Noah and was prophesying of judgment to come upon the wicked people of his time (Jude 14). Just as wicked people tried to kill Moses, Elijah, Jeremiah, Christ and many others who prophesied boldly for God, so Enoch's evil contemporaries tried to kill him. Although God apparently protected him from an untimely death, Enoch ultimately fell asleep even as all the others listed in Hebrews 11.

The word "translated" in Hebrews 11:5 is rendered as "carried over" in Acts 7:16, "removed" in Galatians 1:6 and "changed" in Hebrews 7:12. God moved Enoch from one place to another on the earth so that he would not at that time "see death," that is, "die."

---

[73] Buzzard, op. cit., *What Happens When We Die?*, p. 49.

Psalm 89:48

What man *is he that* liveth, and shall not **see death**? shall he deliver his soul from the hand of the grave?...

Luke 2:26

And it was revealed unto him by the Holy Ghost, that he should not **see death**, before he had seen the Lord's Christ.

Thus he "was not found" by those who sought his life. Nowhere does Scripture say that God at that time gave Enoch everlasting life. Surely by now it is clear that Enoch cannot be one of a select few alive in "heaven."

From another angle, even if Enoch and Elijah were somehow totally unique examples of believers taken bodily to "heaven," this could not be used to prove that any other believer has gone there or anywhere else at his death. As we have seen, a person needs a body in order to be alive. Therefore there is no valid connection between what happened to Enoch and Elijah and what happens to a believer who dies, is buried and rots away. He needs his body raised if he is to live again, and this will not happen until Christ appears.

Revelation 6:9-11

(The souls of them that were slain)

Revelation 6:9-11

(9) And when he had opened the fifth seal, I saw under the altar the souls of them that were slain for the word of God, and for the testimony which they held:

(10) And they cried with a loud voice, saying, How long, O Lord, holy and true, dost thou not judge and avenge our blood on them that dwell on the earth?

(11) And white robes were given unto every one of them; and it was said unto them, that they should rest yet for a little season,

until their fellowservants also and their brethren, that should be killed as they *were*, should be fulfilled.

From these verses it is taught that the "souls" of dead people are alive and speaking. We have seen that in the Bible the word "soul" very often refers to the person himself. Here is another example:

1 Peter 3:20

Which sometime were disobedient, when once the longsuffering of God waited in the days of Noah, while the ark was a preparing, wherein few, that is, **eight souls** [eight people] were saved by water.

Such is the case in Revelation 6:9. The statement simply means, "I saw those [people] who had been slain." How did John "see" them? In the vision that Jesus Christ gave him, recorded in the Book of Revelation, of many future events, including the bodily resurrection of those saints martyred during the period of tribulation. How then did they cry "with a loud voice"? This is the figure of speech called personification. It is:

A figure by which things are represented or spoken of as persons; or, by which we attribute intelligence, by words or actions, to inanimate objects or abstract ideas. [74]

"Inanimate objects" includes dead people. Figuratively, they are represented as alive and waiting, and thus this usage is similar to the usage in Isaiah 14:8-10 noted earlier. Certainly they were not disembodied beings floating around, for how could such wear robes? (For a thorough exposition of Revelation 6:9-11, see E.W. Bullinger's *Commentary On Revelation,* pp. 263-274.)

---

[74] Bullinger, *Figures of Speech In The Bible,* p. 861, Baker Book House, Grand Rapids, MI, Reprinted-1968, Originally Published-1898.

Conclusion

I t should now be obvious that the state of the dead is a compelling and significant subject with many critical ramifications for Christian belief and practice. In the light of Scripture, the "orthodox" Christian Church would be well advised to reconsider its biblically *unorthodox* position on the state of the dead. Those who attempt to lightly dismiss this great truth of God's Word as "soul sleep" or a "cult position" are blatantly avoiding one of Scripture's most important issues.

The Church should consider the scriptural truths that death is the total absence of life, that the pervasive biblical metaphor of "sleep" includes the soul as well as the body and that the dead are "asleep" until they are awakened by Jesus Christ. This is the only doctrine that harmonizes all the biblical evidence in a much more satisfying manner than the common belief that the dead are now alive and conscious in heaven or hell.

Christians would then find themselves better able to promote with full scriptural force the unique bodily resurrection of the Lord Jesus Christ and the coming of Christ as one's only hope for deliverance from the grave. This could have tremendously positive evangelical effects. Such right doctrine in the hearts and on the lips of God's people would also go a long way toward rolling back the relentless forces of darkness that are aggressively promoting universal survival after death—"...Ye shall not surely die."

The dead are truly dead and sleeping in gravedom. Only at the coming of Jesus Christ will those who have believed in Him be made alive forever.

The fact that there is death after life should not unnerve a Christian. Death is like sleep, and we who believe in the Lord Jesus Christ can have total confidence that He will one day appear to raise us and all others who have believed to a glorious and everlasting life.

In the face of Satan's original lie that now permeates nearly every segment of Christendom, let us who do understand and believe the magnificent truth of God's wonderful Word stand squarely, valiantly and boldly upon it. As those deceived by the Adversary are very vocal in their error, let us who love the truth herald it forth with great love for those who need to hear it. As Jesus said, only the truth will make one free. It is our hope that this book goes a long way toward that end.

Scripture Index

Selected Bibliography

Bullinger, E. W. *"Selected Writtings,"*(Johnson Graphics, Decatur, MI), Reprinted 1991.

Burch, Helaine. *"Asleep in Christ;"*(The Open Bible Trust / Bible Search Publications Inc.) 1999.

Buzzard, Anthony. "Life After Death: Resurrection or the Intermediate State?" *A Journal from the Radical Reformation,* Vol. 2, No. 1, 1992.

Buzzard, Anthony. *"What Happens When We Die?,"* (Atlanta Bible College, Morrow, GA), 1986.

Crockett, William (ed.). *"Four Views of Hell,"* (Zondervan Publishing House, Grand Rapids, MI), 1992.

Cullmann, Oscar, *"Immortality of the Soul or Resurrection of the Dead,"* (The Epworth Press, London), 1958.

Eyre, Alan. *"The Protestors,"* (2nd Edition, The Christadelphians, Birmingham, England), 1985.

Froom, LeRoy E. *"The Conditionalist Faith of Our Fathers,"* (Review and Herald Publishing Assn., Washington, D.C.), 1966.

Fudge, Edward. *"The Fire That Consumes,"* (Verdict Press, Fallbrook, CA), 1982.

Hatch, Sidney, *"Daring to Differ:Adventures in Conditional Immortality,"* (Brief Bible Studies, Sherwood, OR).

Ives, Charles. *"The Bible Doctrine of the Soul,"* (Camden, NJ), 1893.

Hewitt, Clyde. *"Midnight and Morning,"* (Venture Books, Charlotte, NC), 1983.

Rawlings, Maurice. *"Before Death Comes,"* (Thomas Nelson, Nashville, TN), 1980.

White, Percy E., *"The Doctrine of the Immortality of the Soul,"* (Christadelphians Scripture Study Services,Torrens Park, South Austrailia).

Wierwille, Victor Paul, *"Are The Dead Alive Now?"* (American Christian Press, New Knoxville, OH), 1973.

What Is Spirit and Truth Fellowship International?

Spirit and Truth Fellowship International is a worldwide community of Christians who desire to make known the written Word of God so as to proclaim the Good News of the Lord Jesus Christ.

The fellowship and community arm of the ministry, including our events and the infrastructure (support services and finances) operates under the banner of *Spirit and Truth Fellowship International*. At the same time, *Christian Educational Services* is the publication and production arm of our ministry. Thus, the organization, like a human body, has two arms with which to reach out.

Our Vision Statement is: "Building a global community of committed Christians living the truth in love."

Our Mission Statement is: "To glorify the One True God and the Lord Jesus Christ by providing sound biblical teaching and a spiritually-empowered fellowship community so that all people may be saved, come to a knowledge of the truth, and become established in faithful and fruitful Christian living."

Spirit and Truth is accomplishing its overall mission by way of live speakers, audio and videotapes, books, and literature, as well as many different kinds of camps and conferences for all ages. Our biblically based teachings point people to the Lordship of Jesus Christ in their lives. The materials produced by Spirit and Truth are designed to assist individual spiritual growth as well as support local fellowships and churches in our Fellowship Community. We encourage Christians to apply these teachings in their local areas in community with other likeminded believers.

Spirit and Truth is composed of an International Headquarters and a worldwide network of independent local groups of Christians around the world. This "Fellowship Community" is made up of believers who freely affiliate themselves with us because they are in agreement with our Statement of Beliefs and Code of Conduct, and have seen the quality of their lives improve by their association with us and what we have to offer. Our goal is to be a "full service" ministry where people can come and find wholeness for themselves, as well as an arena in which to exercise their own unique callings in the Body of Christ.

Our name is partially derived from Jesus' statement in John 4:23 that God is seeking people to worship Him "in spirit and in truth." As that is the only thing stated in Scripture that God seeks, we believe it is imperative that our ministry is oriented to that way of honoring our God. We are a community of worshipers, knit together by the love of God and a common belief of His Word ("the truth"). We seek to empower each believer involved in our ministry to exercise his own unique giftings in accordance with his personal relationship with the Lord Jesus Christ.

The basis for all our efforts is the Bible, which we believe to be the Word of God, perfect in its original writing. So-called errors, contradictions, or discrepancies are the result of man's subsequent interference in the transmission of the text, mistranslations, or failure to understand what is written. We draw from all relevant sources that shed light on the integrity of Scripture, whether in the field of geography, customs, language, history, or principles governing Bible interpretation. Our goal is to seek the truth without respect to tradition or "orthodoxy."

Jesus said that knowing the truth would make one free, and our teachings are oriented to improving one's quality of life. Our goal is to provide healthy biblical teaching that helps people enjoy the fruits of salvation and authentic Christ-like living. When accurately understood, the Word of God brings great deliverance from fear, doubt, and worry, and leads the individual Christian to genuine freedom, confidence, and joy in living. Beyond such practical blessings, however, our goal is to enable each believer to study the Bible for himself so that he is able to develop his own convictions, separate truth from error, and become an effective communicator of God's Word, and successfully live in community with other committed Christians.

What Is Christian Educational Services?

"Christian Educational Services," the original name of our ministry, is the publication and production arm of Spirit and Truth Fellowship International. This includes the research, teaching, and production of books, tapes, videos, and other study and outreach materials.

Any individual willing to examine his beliefs in the light of God's Word can profit from our teachings. They are non-denominational, and are intended to strengthen one's faith in God, Jesus Christ, and the Bible, no matter what his denominational preference may be. Designed primarily for individual home study, the teachings are the result of intensive research and rational methods, making them easy to follow, verify, and practically apply.

To receive our free bimonthly newsletter, *The Sower,* and a complete listing of our materials, please contact us at:

Christian Educational Services
2144 East 52nd Street
Indianapolis, Indiana 46205
888-255-6189, M-F 8:30 to 5
CES@CESonline.org
www.CESonline.org

We look forward to hearing from you!

Further Study Material

Other Books, Publications, and Seminars, available from
Christian Educational Services
2144 East 52nd Street
Indianapolis, Indiana 46205
888-255-6189, M-F 8:30 to 5
Jesusces@aol.com
www.CESonline.org

Books

One God & One Lord: Reconsidering The Cornerstone of the Christian Faith

The Christian's Hope: The Anchor of the Soul – What the Bible really says about Death, Judgment, Rewards, Heaven, and the Future Life on a Restored Earth

The Gift of Holy Spirit: Every Christian's Divine Deposit

Don't Blame God! A Biblical Answer to the Problem of Evil, Sin, and Suffering

Sex & Scripture: A Biblical Study of Proper Sexual Behavior

Publications

The Bible—You Can Believe It

Righteousness: Every Christian's Gift from God

Beyond a Reasonable Doubt—23 Arguments for the Historical Validity of the Resurrection of Jesus Christ

22 Principles of Bible Interpretation or How to Eliminate Apparent Bible Contradictions

23 Reasons to Believe in a Rapture before the Great Tribulation or Why We Aren't in the Tribulation Now

25 Reasons Why Salvation is Permanent for Christians

34 Reasons Why the Holy Spirit is Not a Separate "Person" From the Only True God, The Father
46 Reasons Why our Heavenly Father has no Equals or "Co-Equals"

Defending Dispensationalism: Standing Fast in the Liberty

Becoming a Christian: Why? What? How?

The Death Penalty: Godly or Ungodly?

Audio Tape Seminars

New Life in Christ—Foundations for Powerful Christian Living (15 hrs)

Growing Up in Christ, Part One: The Fruit of the Spirit— Developing the Character of Christ (12 hrs)

Growing Up in Christ, Part Two: Teaching and Activation in the Manifestations of the Gift of Holy Spirit (9 hrs)

A Journey through the Old Testament (26 hrs)

Romans (18 hrs)

The Book of Revelation (9 hrs)

Jesus Christ, the Diameter of the Ages (6 hrs)

Truth or Tradition? (12 hrs)

The Creation-Evolution Controversy (6 hrs)

Dating, Courtship, & Engagment: A Journey in Preparing For Marriage ($2^{1/2}$ hrs)

**For further study on this subject,
be sure to visit our research website:**

ww.TruthorTradition.com

A website dedicated to helping you understand
the Word of God, free from the tradition of men.